HOT RODS AND CUSTOM CARS

OF THE

SACRAMENTO DELTA

HOT RODS AND CUSTOM CARS

OF THE

SACRAMENTO DELTA

JOHN V. CALLAHAN

THE
History
PRESS

Published by The History Press
Charleston, SC
www.historypress.com

First published 2019

Manufactured in the United States

ISBN 9781467139953

Library of Congress Control Number: 2018960965

THIS BOOK IS DEDICATED to Lenny Byer (1933–2010). Lenny was a customizer of cars and hot rods who was as good as any in that field and became famous. He invented his creation of a custom lacquer paint formula called Candy Apple Red. The paint was the first of its kind to have a deep, brilliant red, the color of the candy apple you bought at the carnival. Joe Bailon, the original inventor of the color, said:

There are only three painters who can paint Candy Apple Red: Joe Bailon, George Barris and Lenny Byer, the 3 Bs.

I remember visiting his shop at Bauman Motors after school, and he let me hang around. Lenny Byer was a good guy who let us watch him work and answered our curious questions. There always seemed to be someone around after school to check out what was going on. It was a great experience to see a master at work. He had some guys who worked for him that were also talented, including Doug Morden, George Amaral and Walt Schmit.

CONTENTS

Acknowledgements 11
Introduction 13

I. THE BUILDERS AND CUSTOMIZERS

Lenny Byer: Legendary Customizer 21
Harry Westergard: Master of Sheet Metal 26
Rico Squalia: 1923 Ford Roadster Track T,
      America's Most Beautiful Roadster 1951 28
Dennis Lesh: Hot Rod and Motorcycle Builder 37
Tom Cutino: Master of the Art 40
Lucky Silva: Hot Rods, Motorcycles and Custom Cars 47
Manny Fernandez: 1940 Mercury 50
Walt "Waldo" Schmit: 1957 Ford Fairlane 54
Jack Coughlin: 1932 Roadster Highboy 60
Ron "Boots" Heath: 1932 Ford Roadster, Wildfire Pickup,
      1936 Ford 65
Dave Dias: 1928 Ford Roadster Pickup 70
Dale "Slim" Kamen: America's Most Beautiful Roadster 74

II. THE CARS

Harry Hansen: 1952 Chevrolet Hardtop 79
Bobby Hadden: 1950 Ford Coupe 82

CONTENTS

Bill Cabral: 1954 Ford/1958 Oldsmobile ... 84
Wayne Culp: 1950 Mercury ... 87
Edward "Tippee" Del Charo: 1960 Oldsmobile ... 90
Ron Debasco: 1955 Chevrolet ... 91
Rod Dolk: 1934 Ford Pickup ... 93
Bob Dron: 1950 Chevrolet Hardtop ... 97
Don Dozier: 1949 Chevrolet Four-Door ... 99
Randy Fernandez: 1956 Chevrolet Two-Door Post ... 102
Joey and Frank Ferreira: 1923 Ford Roadster,
    America's Most Beautiful Roadster ... 103
Nini Fevereiro: 1950 Chevrolet Coupe/1955 Chevrolet Hardtop ... 105
Bob Fritts: 1958 Chevrolet Impala ... 109
Arnold Gouveia: 1955 Ford Convertible/1923 Ford Roadster ... 111
George Lira: 1923 Ford Roadster Pickup ... 113
Lyle Jessee: 1950 Oldsmobile Rocket 88 ... 115
Norman "Wally" Marks: 1955 Chevrolet ... 117
Walt Roselini: 1950 Ford ... 119
Ernie Lucas: 1963 Dodge/1939 Chevrolet Coupe ... 120
Jim Morris: 1951 Chevrolet Hardtop ... 123
Twig Silva: 1923 Ford Panel ... 126
Charlie Scholting: C&S Auto Parts ... 128
Doug Schafer: 1954 Chevrolet Pickup ... 129
Jack Schafer: 1932 Ford Five-Window Coupe ... 132
Thom Smith: 1954 Chevrolet/1934 Ford Roadster ... 136
Al and Jane Thurman: 1931 Ford Sedan ... 139
Le and Robby Weber: 1941 Ford Sedan Delivery ... 143
Darryl Batchelor: 1923 Ford T Roadster ... 145
Ezra Ehrhardt: California Highway Patrol ... 147

III. CAR CLUBS AND CAR SHOWS

The Gear Jammers, Rio Vista ... 149
The Levee Lopers, Rio Vista ... 149
The Delta-Creepers, Isleton ... 149
The Rio Vista Bass Derby and Car Show ... 150
Kingdon Drag Strip, Lodi, California ... 151
Model Car Shows ... 153
Rio Vista High School Auto Shop Club ... 158
Get Together Pictures, Around the Delta ... 159

CONTENTS

Epilogue   165

Glossary   167

Bibliography   171

About the Author   173

ACKNOWLEDGEMENTS

I have read that writing is a lonely art. I guess that depends on who and what you are writing about. My subject is cars and people, but not ordinary cars or people. This book came about because memories aren't always exactly the way we remember them. I personally know the majority of people and cars spotlighted here, and their help in clarifying many things is beyond my ability to express. Also, some published articles are included because the excellent stories told it better than I could. Each is credited before their story. The conversations I've had with car people reveal their interest has never diminished a bit. Guys like Tom Cutino are still turning out customs at our advanced age because the interest worldwide is still growing. Television shows about car builders are popular. Just to mention a few:

Boyd Coddington's Garage (in syndication)
Dave Kindig's Bitchin' Rides
Jay Leno's Garage
Inside West Coast Customs
Chip Foose's Overhauling
Wayne Carini's Chasing Classic Cars

There are many more out there, and the number would be near impossible to count. There are major shows, but city and state shows in a local, one- or two-day smaller format are everywhere. They use entry fees to support charities in their areas. Great cars and owners who support local causes make these worthy events.

INTRODUCTION

You need to be a local and real aficionado of custom cars and hot rods to know who some of the people mentioned in this book are. Back in the 1950s, hot rod building and street racing were widespread and mostly illegal, sort of the Wild West phase of their history. The Delta is as flat as a pancake, with roads elevated a bit to keep the farms from the river. The roads are dangerous, twisting every which way. Teenagers were pretty much sequestered at home unless they had driver's licenses. Farm kids could get an early driver's license if they could qualify for one. The school bus was their major means of transportation, commuting to and from school. A car became a necessity just to survive, and regardless what kind of car a teenage boy got, he wanted to fix it up. Many learned their automotive skills welding and fixing farm equipment. Harvesters and other machinery needed to run and get fixed immediately, or crops could fail. But these teenagers didn't want Dad's truck to drive to school, they wanted their own cars fixed up their own ways. Hot rodding in the early days had a bad name, street racing was out of control and the publicity that came with it was bad. Fortunately, many cars were available if you could keep them running, but that wasn't good enough. It had to be your car, changed to what you wanted—and what you wanted would be different than anyone else's. There was another added benefit: meeting girls! If you had a cool car, you could cruise around town, maybe go to Sacramento or Stockton. There were numerous hangouts like the A&W drive-in, Bob's or Granny's drive-ins in Rio Vista and other towns. These were pretty much the local hangouts, and out-of-town places were at least an hour away along levee roads. Thanks to the California Highway Patrol (CHP) and other sources, organized car clubs and positive publicity, attitudes changed as hot rods and custom cars gained maturity and acceptance; certain people gained respect for their contributions and the fame that went along with it. The Sacramento Delta was fortunate to have a few who fit that bill. Two notables were Harry Westergard and Rico Squalia, who both lived and worked between Isleton and Walnut Grove. They are still remembered today, Harry for his genius of metal forming and Rico for his mechanic skills. Together they made a famous hot rod. There are many others who are remembered for their cars that were family and personal transportation. They drove what they created, rolling art, unfinished in many cases, but loved as their own. When we talk about someone whose name we can't remember, a description of his car identified him immediately—it's a rolling ID card.

THE HOT ROD CRAZE

A hot rod craze was sweeping the nation in the years after World War II, and California was the place to be if cars were your passion. Los Angeles and the Pacific Coast Highway drew most of the attention from the newspapers and magazine articles—in some ways, negative publicity. Wild teenagers in motion pictures like *The Wild One*, *Hot Rod Girl*, *Hot Rods to Hell*, *The Wild Ride* and *Hot Rod Rumble* represented Hollywood cashing in on the growing culture. Even Elvis Presley, in *Loving You*, drove a black open-wheeled Ford Model A hot rod with a flathead engine and dual carbs. Looking back, it's not hard to understand our elders' reaction to hot rods when they saw the films and read reviews in the papers of illegal street racing. Locally, cars were racing around the narrow Delta two-lane roads, which were dangerous under normal traffic. Out of the bad publicity and public view came the effort to bring legitimacy to the culture. The kids interested in cars formed car clubs to try to get their parents' approval and do some good deeds in the community. They were helped along the way by the California Highway Patrol. The following article appeared in the Wednesday, February 24, 1960, issue of the *River News Herald*:

Hot Rodders Termed among the Best Drivers by Authority

The public owes Hot Rodders an apology and a debt of gratitude, so says Wally Parks, president of the National Hot Rod Association, who is editor of Hot Rod Magazine. *Hot Rodder is generally associated by the public with any teenager who drives recklessly, but according to Parks most true hot rodders might give the average driver a lesson in good driving. In a true sense of the word, "Hot Rodder" applies to any youth who is a member of a car club. Most of these clubs are either a member or modeled after a club that belongs to the NHRA. All members are required to pay half the amount of any fine received for a traffic violation to their club and may be expelled. These clubs are made up of youths who are interested in cars, not only for speed but for safety and mechanical perfection and unique styling as well. Most Hot Rodders are interested in racing their cars, but in the majority of their racing activity are confined to authorized and supervised drag strips. It is the youths who do not belong to such clubs that give young drivers a bad name. To quote Johnnie Parsons, veteran racing driver, and holder of two championships: "Hot Rodders and sports car enthusiasts are the safest drivers on the road today. They know more about driving, take better care of their cars and more consideration for other drivers than the average person behind the wheel today."*

Many components of today's passenger cars were originated in a trial and error process by members of hot rod clubs. Such a club is the Rio Vista Levee Lopers which has been in existence for a little more than four years. A self-supporting organization of the club has 13 members at the present time. Meetings are held each Monday at 8:00 p.m. under the supervision of Bob Simons and Calvin Krienke. The official insignia of the club is a striped bass leaping out of the water with the carburetors and exhaust headers exiting the gills. When the club originated the first meetings were held in the basement of the Charles Tudhope home. Young George Tudhope was the first president of the Levee Lopers. At present the club is meeting in a building owned by the Blackwelder Company and has been granted the use if some of the Blackwelder equipment. The club's main project at the present time is the building of a Chrysler powered B pickup which the members anticipate having finished by spring. The vehicle will be run at sanctioned drag races when it has been completed. Dances, held usually once a month, are the club's only means of fund raising and are held at the Youth Center. These dances are chaperoned by two or more members of the Soroptimist Club which has presented them with the needed equipment

*and who furnish cookies and the punch that is served during the evening.
The stigma connected with the term hot rodder is being banished somewhat
when nine times out of ten that young man that stops to help a motorist in
trouble proves to be a member of a hot rod club. He will not accept payment
for his service but will always leave his card telling the grateful motorist
he is indebted to a hot rodder. There were other car clubs around the delta
past and present:*

*The Gear Jammers, Rio Vista
The Delta-Creepers, Isleton
The Clutchers Car Club, Courtland
The Delta Drifters, Antioch
The Levee Lopers, Rio Vista
The Road Angels, Lodi*

The cars in this book are memories. Each one was a dream of the owner,
a process from beginning to end that took a real physical form. You could
drive it anywhere you wanted to go, with each step of building in view
of everyone. That view was mostly paint primer. Ornamental chrome on
the body was routinely removed, leaded and prepared to paint. Budgets
commanded the amount you spent on a project, but money doesn't always
make a bad design better.

The Sacramento Delta reflects a pie-shaped area of land and islands
approximately 1,100 square miles, 500,000 acres and 57 islands. It's a spider
web of two-lane roads that follow the Sacramento River on its journey to
the San Francisco Bay. Highway 160 wanders south from the state capital
to the town of Freeport, where the delta begins. The river twists down
to Clarksburg, passing west of Hood to Courtland and continuing south
as we pass Walnut Grove to Isleton, until we reach the largest city: Rio
Vista. In 1960, Rio Vista had a population of around 2,600 and Isleton
around 1,050. These small towns were far from the metropolitan cities
that surrounded the Southern California area with more kids, cars and
entertainment. Our area was mostly farmland. The delta was a result of
decaying marsh vegetation that made a foundation of peat soil. It is a rich
soil that has a year-round fresh water supply. Many of the hot rods and
custom cars came from residents living with addresses starting with a route
number. These were farm families living near the crops they produced:
corn, milo, alfalfa, pears, wheat, barley, potatoes and various other crops
that were started and failed over the century. Farm kids were able to use

skills developed in their shops maintaining farm equipment to support the family. Americas Most Beautiful Roadster began as a body and trunk abandoned in a cow pasture on Tyler Island. Rod Dolk's 1934 Ford pickup came from a ranch on Ryer Island. This was the 1950s and '60s, the early days of what has become an enormous empire. What is truly unique is that both of these homemade hot rods still run, and their owners remain within fifteen miles of their Delta hometowns.

The city of Rio Vista is located in the lower part of the Delta and is not on an island. It is in an area known as the Montezuma Hills. It is separated from the rich peat soil to its east by the mile-wide Sacramento River. The river widens even more as it joins the San Joaquin River at Sherman Island and flows through the Carquinez Strait and drains into the San Francisco Bay.

Rio Vista is situated in a very fortunate area. It is blessed with a great waterway that brings fishermen from all parts of the world. It supports striped bass, sturgeon and catfish for sport fishermen and also is popular for water skiing and parasailing. Natural gas was discovered in the Montezuma Hills to the south in 1936. It is one of the largest reserves of dry gas in the nation. The gas pipe lines go north nearly five miles and turn to the river. West, they bulge five miles and then taper another eight miles to the south. A single pipeline crosses east to the river and under the Sandy Beach area to Brannon Island. The pipeline spreads out a couple of miles east and south to Sherman Island. From the sky, it doesn't look like a huge area in size, but that is made up by the volume of natural gas it contains. The impact on the community was tremendous. The jobs it brought to the area increased the population, and support businesses made the city a popular place to live. When World War II began, the fields became even more important to our military effort. After the war, soldiers, sailors and airmen returned home to the Delta, and they were the first to start our hot rod culture. There is now another relatively new addition to the Montezuma Hills: giant wind turbines, over 750 of them from Rio Vista to Collinsville, about ten miles on a route that follows along the path of the Sacramento River. So, there it is: natural resources and unnatural structures combining to bring prosperity to the Delta. It also gave the youth jobs to pay for their cars, to customize and equip their hot rods with bigger engines.

PART I

THE BUILDERS AND CUSTOMIZERS

LENNY BYER

LEGENDARY CUSTOMIZER

Lenny T. Byer came to Rio Vista in the early 1950s. He was born in Farmington, Arkansas, on January 5, 1933, and moved to Brentwood, California, when he was eight years old. He graduated from Liberty High School in 1951. He was drafted in 1953 into the U.S. Army and sent by ship from New York to Italy. After Byer waited there for three weeks, the army sent him to Salzburg, Austria, where he was assigned as a chief cook for his unit. Lenny served his two years' enlistment and left the army as a sergeant. He returned home and married his high school sweetheart, Joanne.

He began working as a body shop man in a car dealership. He learned how to do the basic things everyone in the automobile repair trade knows. One must learn to bring bent, busted cars back to original condition. Along the way, he learned to work with the lead that was used as body filler.

Lenny Byer is remembered as Byer's, not Byer, by many. Why, it just sounded good when bragging about the work he did to one's car. It seemed to carry a natural sound when explaining the work done to your ride. It usually started by the nearest primer spot on the body metal. Words were used that you wouldn't understand unless you dug the lingo. *Primered, channeled, chopped, leading, raked* and *drag pipes* were commonly understood, and Lenny was an expert at applying these things to whatever you brought to his shop. He worked in Rio Vista and commuted daily home across the mile-wide bridge, south along the two-lane winding levee road along the Sacramento River. He went along Brannon Island to Sherman Island and over the Antioch bridge to his home in Oakley. At times, he commuted with Doug Morden, who worked with him at Bauman Motors, where he ran the body shop, and again later when Byer had a shop in Brentwood.

He told me that the car pictured below was his first ever custom project. It started as a 1927 turtleback Ford and became an art deco classic. It was a popular style in the '30s and continued until after World War II. Popular cars of the time like Cords, LaSalles and fabulous Auburn Speedsters are still in style today. It was the first true hot rod he ever built. Those early roadsters were solid yet somewhat bulky in appearance. They needed to be sturdy, as they were also used for daily transportation. The hand-formed front end with its cow catcher–style front bumper and sleek rounded nose flowing to the louvered hood and snap down side panels were all smoothed to the body lines. The interior is a tucked and padded leather rolled over the body and features a huge steering wheel. The windshield had chopped posts that hold the elegantly curved windshield that also matches and supports the curl of the cowl and instrument panel. The turtleback rear end was molded to fit the curve on the back of the "T" body. Moving down are unique fenders. They cover about half of the wheels and were actually spare tire covers that

Car show at the Bass Derby in Rio Vista. Wildfire is displayed with everything open. This is customizing at its finest. *Callahan Collection.*

Lenny Byer working on the hood of a '55 Chevy using lead applied with a torch and wood paddle to fill in gaps and molding in. *Courtesy of Danny Kamen.*

Lenny Byer's personal street rod roadster on display at the Oakland Roadster Show. It was a class winner in the category. *Courtesy of the Byer Collection.*

were customized to follow the theme of the car. Big, fat, whitewall tires and full hubcaps were also blended in to the rest of the car. The frame is visible and very powerful, mounting the chromed wishbone supports that attach to the front and rear axles, keeping it in proper alignment. This is one of the finest examples of the elegance that was brought into the world of hot rods, demonstrating that true style was not just for high-end factory cars. They are numerous, but this was a one-of-a-kind Concours d'Elegance vehicle.

Lenny went to work in Rio Vista at Bauman Motors and began doing body shop work. He worked for Jack Bauman, who was a man of vision for the town. Bauman not only owned the Ford dealership but also developed a small canal running south of town called St. Joseph's Cut. When he bought the canal, he turned it into Delta Marina, and built a restaurant named "the Point." Jack Bauman saw local kids wanting to customize their cars, and Lenny Byer had the knowledge and experience to do just what they needed done. They sold new cars and had a used car lot, and that worked for parents and kids. Bauman encouraged Byer to do the customizing for the kids because they would eventually marry and need family transportation. Their loyalty would mean more business. For example, customer Harry Hansen wanted a car to compete in one of the biggest car shows in the country: the Oakland National Car Show. This would lead to the major transformation of his '52 Chevy hardtop.

One of the achievements Lenny was able to accomplish was to figure out how to re-create Candy Apple Red paint. It was invented by Joe Bailon, a famous Bay Area customizer who won fame by inventing the process to paint the deep beautiful color. Lenny told me the story of how it happened: After work was done for the day, he and other workers would go outside the shop and have a cold beer. Their chairs were near the edge of the Sacramento River, and the beer of choice was Lucky Lager in a can. It has a beautiful gold color base with a big red X on the label. What he noticed was the red was translucent. He began testing the combination of different shades of gold and red until he got everything right: Candy Apple Red. Harry Hansen's '52 Chevy was one of his best paint jobs; a paint job can be truly great only when it is applied correctly with coat after coat and color sanded each time until it is perfect. Since this is a two-stage application, the second color, translucent red, is applied until the layers of color to reach the desired shade. It is finished with clear glossy lacquer until the coolest color ever is achieved. This is what Lenny Byer did.

While he transformed many cars and roadsters, there was only one car on which he did a total full customizing job. It was a 1950 four-door Ford called

At a car show in full display is the four-door '50 Ford of Ron Puccinelli. He proudly shows the unusual door configuration by opening the back door, rather than hiding it. Very good planning. *Courtesy of the Byer Collection.*

the Majestic Lady. There are, of course, many four-door cars that have been in numerous car shows, but not so much in the top shows. Lenny said it was the only four-door he ever customized. It is shown here in the Oakland National Roadster Show in full regalia. The angel hair surrounding the car had two purposes: a nice setting around the car, and it does not allow the judges to look under the vehicle and find flaws. It was painted gold, with many features like frenched headlights, a new grille and drag pipes with special housing split so doors would open and new taillights and bumper. The interior was velvet with buttons and bucket seats.

HARRY WESTERGARD

MASTER OF SHEET METAL

You have to be a real car aficionado to know who Harry Westergard was and his contribution to hot rods and custom cars. I admit I knew little about him until I started my research for this story. Harry was creative beyond any fabricator who used the English Wheel to roll and shape sheet metal. He was an area guy, born and raised in Sacramento, California. Little is known about his early years except he always hung around Browns Body Shop, where he learned the basics of body work and welding. Westergard became an employee along with another young kid who liked to hang out at the body shop like he did. George Barris was that young man, and he and his brother Sam learned body work from Harry. We know where Barris went from there. Some guys were getting together to form a car club, and he joined in, becoming a founding member of the Capitol Auto Club, which met at Harry Westergard's home on Fulton Avenue. As time went by and things changed, the club evolved to become the "Thunderbolts." It is still in existence today. Westergard enlisted in the U.S. Navy and returned home after his hitch was completed. He returned to Sacramento and resumed customizing cars.

One day, Harry met a young man at a Capitol Auto Club meeting named Butler Rugard from Walnut Grove, down the river. Harry went south to work for Rico Squalia in Walnut Grove and lived in a place behind the shop.

Butler wanted Harry to build him a custom car, and one turned into two builds. The first was a '47, and the second, more famous, was a '40 Mercury. The '40 was the big undertaking, and it was a brand-new car just off the dealer's floor. This was a unique effort, since few could afford to drive it off the showroom floor and into the auto shop. It was also big project, including a top chop and conversion to a Carson style. Westergard was also known for extending front fenders to the rear ones in a fade-away style. This style was adopted by Detroit several years later. Harry had done work on Rico's '23 T, creating the hood, Curtis-style nose and grille and a full belly pan. It was awarded America's Most Beautiful Roadster in 1951. It was also entered in the first Sacramento Car Show. Unfortunately, Harry Westergard was killed in an automobile crash while heading north to Sacramento. The extremely dangerous, narrow, winding road claimed another victim—and not the last. Once, a customer looking to buy a '40 Merc called a friend, famous car builder George Barris, to ask if he should buy it since he said it was made by Westergard. George asked if it had fade-away fenders and push button door opener; he said it did. George had a two-word answer: "BUY IT."

RICO SQUALIA

1923 FORD ROADSTER TRACK T, AMERICA'S MOST BEAUTIFUL ROADSTER 1951

Isleton, California, is a small town in the central Sacramento Delta. Rico Squalia was one of the most talented custom car builders and an innovator of that era. His first hot rod was an open-wheeled racetrack-style roadster built in 1948. It was built by hand at the Studebaker dealership he owned with partner Jack Sean. A September 1951 article in *Hot Rod Magazine* said this about Rico:

After studying the street roadsters featured in Hot Rod Magazine *and displayed at several car roadster shows he decided to enter this phase of hot rodding. These were the days of using existing parts from manufactured vehicles and those you created. As a mechanic and fabricator, he decided to scratch-build a car himself. As the story goes, the roadster was started in 1948, when Rico located a 1923 Ford model T body and turtleback trunk. It was found abandoned in a cow pasture on Tyler Island and brought in to his shop on a flat-bed truck. Rico designed the roadster in the popular style of the day: race cars. As a welder and mechanic who drew plans and knew how to bring them to life. His first design was the frame which he made 3 ½" by 2" channel iron with chrome alloy steel tubing. He found and installed a Ford model B front axle and rear end with a '23 T spring. The body had a lot of weathering and rust and was cleaned up and sanded. The body was then channeled 4" and mounted to the frame. Channeling is lowering the body by moving the floor pan up, so the body rides lower on the frame. Rico turned to an artistic metalworker who became famous for his*

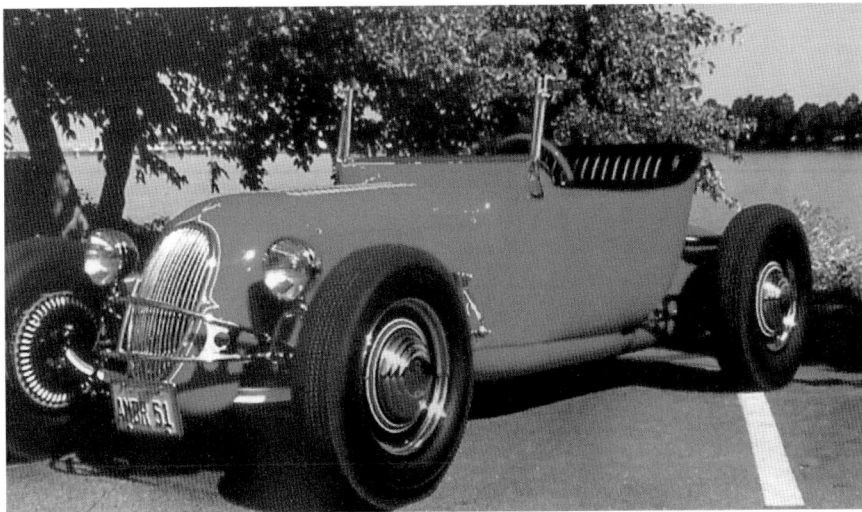

After all the changes and modifications, this track T-style roadster is a tribute to Dennis Lesh's skill and talent of building cars from scratch. *Courtesy of the Lesh Collection.*

customizing: Harry Westergard. Harry was working on the hood shell to flow from the cowl to the rounded nose grille. He worked with an English Wheel, a metalworking tool that makes compound curves from flat sheets of metal such as aluminum or steel.

Louvers were added in three rows on the top of the hood and two rows on the side panels. Harry also formed the entire under-body, full-length belly pan. It was then gas welded, hammered, dollied, leaded and prepped for the final paint. This was the period of real fabricators who worked with metal. Rico was responsible for all the mechanical work, including building the suspension, electrical wiring, transmission and the hopped-up 1941 Mercury flathead V8-60 engine. The body was pieced back together and the handmade front and rear nerf bar bumpers, chromed, of course. The final finish body work was done by Dale "Slim" Kamen, another Isleton resident. For paint, they chose a 1944 Packard Matador Red. The interior was finished in classic black tuck and roll by Bob and Marion Upholstery of Sacramento. The roadster was completed in time for the second Oakland National Roadster Show. "Others are larger, and perhaps more specular, but the Oakland National Show remains hot rodding's national shrine," said Tex Smith. The show ran for six days, February

Close-up of the front end of Rico Squalia's America's Most Beautiful Roadster. This is what it looks like coming down the opposite lane toward you. *Courtesy of the Squalia Collection.*

20–25, 1951, at the Oakland Exposition Building across from Lake Merritt in downtown Oakland, California.

It was the second show; the first drew 27,624 fans. Rico Squalia brought the roadster by trailer and rolled it into the building because the motor was not finished. This was not to be a problem, because there were no rules in place to disqualify a car for that reason. After the show, that rule would be changed, and the new rule clearly stated that every car in the show had to be driven into the building and then driven out. The one

The Oakland National Roadster showroom floor with the nine-foot trophy presented for the winner. Rico Squalia's roadster would claim that prize and display it for a year. *Courtesy of the Squalia Collection.*

thing that was outstanding about Squalia's entry was the overall design. The roadster is right in every respect; every part works harmoniously, and it is well balanced and pleasingly whole. It just fits together perfectly. The results of the judges' voting proved that, as it became Americas Most Beautiful Roadster.

J.C. "Aggie" Agajanian, one of the most influential figures in American motorsports history, presented Rico Squalia with his personal trophy. Agajanian is famous from his cars in the Indianapolis 500 and as a member of the Motor Sports Hall of Fame.

Winning the nine-foot trophy brought one more little-known commitment: you must also take it home with you to display and return it to the next year's show. That was easy, since Rico was now head mechanic at the Fran Awalt Ford dealership in Walnut Grove, California. It was proudly displayed in the main showroom. Many people stopped by the dealership because it was on the major road, Highway 160, to Sacramento from Delta towns.

Left: J.C. Agajanian presents Rico Squalia with one of the four trophies awarded at the show. Rico's son Ricky still has them. *Courtesy of the Squalia Collection.*

Below: Rico Squalia with the roadster at Fran Alwalt's Ford dealership in Walnut Grove with his trophies. The nine-foot trophy was displayed in the front showroom for one year until the next show. He kept the four smaller trophies for his collection. *Courtesy of the Squalia Collection.*

Rico s its on the base of the nine-foot trophy surrounded by trophies and fans. *Courtesy of the Squalia Collection.*

It was the intent of the Oakland National Roadster Show committee that a winner's display would help promote and advertise next year's show.

On the cover of the September 1951 issue of *Hot Rod Magazine,* two vehicles are pictured. One is a streamlined Bonneville-style land speed record racecar that featured twin side-by-side engines. The second picture is Rico Squalia's 1923 Ford T roadster in color. It was quite an accomplishment for a hand-built car from Isleton, California, to be featured on the cover of a nationally published magazine. Rico kept the roadster until 1957, when he sold it to August "Auggie" Correia for $700. He drove it around locally and enjoyed it as a family car. He sold the roadster to the Ferreira brothers, Joey and Frank.

Time passed, and the roadster was disassembled and put in boxes and stored in a garage in Isleton. In 1985, Joey ran into a friend, Carter Fisher, and the casual conversation led him to ask Carter if he was still interested in buying the car for $1,500. Carter immediately said yes, and the deal was made. Carter is a very good mechanic and metal worker and would have those skills put to an extreme test.

HOT ROD

MAGAZINE

SEPTEMBER 1951
25c

NITRO — The Poor Man's Supercharger

TWIN - ENGINE CUTAWAY

See Pages 26-27

America's Most Beautiful Roadster on the cover of *Hot Rod* magazine. It was quite an accomplishment for Rico Squalia to achieve the fame of being on the cover and featured inside. *From* Hot Rod Magazine, *September 1951.*

A levee break in 1972 flooded 35 percent of Isleton, and the garage where the roadster was stored received some damage. Carter did the majority of the restoration himself. His shop is seven miles north of Isleton in Ryde, a town consisting of a post office, a hotel and a bar. Just across the intersecting road is Carter's workshop/garage. The eastern view from the garage is a two-lane road and levee bank to the Sacramento River. The traffic is intermittent and pretty quiet; few ever stop unless it's their destination. He brought all the parts to the shop and, after careful examination and further disassembling, began restoration. The undercarriage was a mess of numerous welds and multiple drill holes that had to be grinded, filled and rewelded. The entire body, belly pan and hood/grille were in bad shape—not to mention the nerf bar bumpers. Work was slow, and one day he received a call from the Grand Nation Roadster Show asking him if he could show the car at the fifty-year reunion. The show was to feature America's Most Beautiful Roadster past winners. That would only allow him nine months to finish it. With determination, he worked night and day and weekends to complete the job. He also learned how to chrome and did it himself. The roadster was on display at the 2017 Grand National Roadster Show in Pomona and also at the Sacramento Autorama.

Arguably the most notable and famous hot rod that came from the Delta was the 1923 T Ford roadster. In May 2010, Chris Shelton wrote a story about it in *Rod & Custom*:

> *People seem to forget about Seconds even if they're winners in their own right. For example, chances are you wouldn't have to look far if you wanted to know who won America's Most Beautiful Roadster (née World's) at the inaugural Grand National Roadster Show. It seems everybody knows that Bill Niekamp won the first spot on the big trophy in 1950. But you'd have to ask quite a few more people if you wanted to know who won that title the following year. And if you got an answer at all it would probably come from a guy with wispy white hair and yellowing glasses. Even then he'd probably squint into the distance and bring his hand up to bob his index finger as if he was parting cards in an internal Rolodex. And if his cards were still stacked right, he'd say Rico Squalia won that year with a Matador Red '23 Ford roadster.*

Rico's son Rick still lives in the small Delta town of Walnut Grove, California. The current population is about 1,500, but it grows a bit in the boating season. The Sacramento River flows directly through the center of the town on its way to the San Francisco Bay. It is here and in nearby towns that the legendary roadster was built and remains. Rick still has most of his dad's original car show trophies. The one he does not have is the nine-foot-tall monster trophy engraved with the names of the previous winners—that one is still in circulation. The trophy resides in storage these days since it is sixty-seven years old. It is still awarded each year to America's Most Beautiful Roadster, with the winner's name engraved on it.

DENNIS LESH

HOT ROD AND MOTORCYCLE BUILDER

Dennis was creative. This is what customizing is, modifying something to meet individual or personal specifications. He built many cars, motorcycles and trucks in his shop in Rio Vista behind Oilwell Materials. I would stop in to see him whenever I was in town. He always had work because he was good at his trade.

His shop was clean, with a steady clientele. It was usually neat and swept up at night. It also was a gathering place for car guys. Work was always going on, and since Dennis liked to go to car shows, the journey usually began there. He usually drove his current build, either car or motorcycle. They were made to drive and not be just show cars, and he proved that himself.

Dennis's 1927 T track roadster was rebuilt a couple of times. First, it had a partial hood with a 283 Chevy engine with ram's horn manifold exhaust underneath to rear tailpipes. Then he changed it into a more competitive look by changing engines to a 350-cubic-inch Chevy with two fours with tunnel rams. The headers were from Sanderson Sprint series and came over the frame and down the body. This cuts down the backpressure because all the pipes are exactly the same length. The exhaust gasses arrive at the collector (a larger

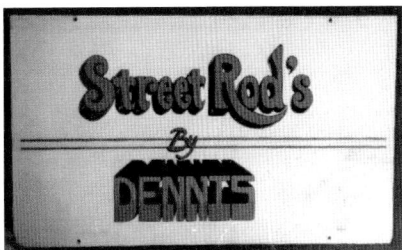

The sign for his custom car body shop was plain and simple: Street Rods by Dennis. It says just what he wanted to it to say. *Courtesy of the Lesh Collection.*

Dennis Lesh sits on Tom Cutino's street roadster pickup at a Goodguys car show in Pleasanton, California. *Courtesy of the Lesh Collection.*

A view from above of the shop, nothing fancy, but laid out and maintained in proper order. Unlike many other shops' appearance, his is clean and orderly. *Courtesy of the Lesh Collection.*

An in-process shot of the Dennis Lesh '28 roadster. It has a different engine and hood that were changed when finished. *Courtesy of the Lesh Collection.*

pipe) at the same time and give more power to the engine. The body is a one-piece polyform with sprint-style nose cut to a perfect fit. The interior (second one) was stitched in nearby Fairfield at Browns Upholstery. The wheels are Centerline Modular Convo Pro satin finish. The finish paint was Hugger Orange racing.

TOM CUTINO

MASTER OF THE ART

Tom Cutino came to live in Rio Vista after high school in Monterey, California. When he started customizing his first car, a shoebox 1950 Ford two-door sedan, he was working out of his backyard. Tom bought it completely stock in Isleton for $1,500. He said he never wanted anything stock, so he started customizing it. Tom laid out the complete plans to follow during construction.

He started by chopping the top four inches in twenty-four hours with gas welding using coat hanger wire. It took a gallon of Bondo filler to finish that job. The slanted mid-post is aligned with the roof slant. The emblems were all removed, and a modification was made to the grille, making the center into a bullet made from a '36 Ford headlight bucket upside down. The stock headlights were replaced with '54 Mercs and stock taillights both frenched. A guard was added to the rear bumper from a '55 Pontiac. Tom painted the car a Corvette yellow separated at the body molding to a brown lower area. The interior was stitched in light brown with velour inserts. It's powered by a V-8 flathead and three-speed overdrive transmission. It was finished with twin Appleton spotlights, full-length drag pipes, fat whitewall tires and moon hubcaps with six pyramid spinners.

Down the road a few years, Tom decided to modify the look of the Ford. It was repainted Pearl White overall with Garnet Red scallops. The grille was reshaped to fit a DeSoto grille, and the hood corners were also reshaped and rounded to fit.

Tom Cutino's custom 1952 Ford in front of his home on Virginia Drive, where he built the car in his backyard. The top was chopped along with most body work. *Courtesy of Tom Cutino.*

Tom Cutino on the road with Dennis Lesh, going to Oakland to put it in the Oakland Roadster Show. *Photo by Dennis Lesh, courtesy of Tom Cutino.*

Tom Cutino's car on display at the Oakland Roadster Show. It was opened up for inspection of the attendees' and the critical judging. *Courtesy of Tom Cutino.*

This is the same '50 gold Ford after Tom Cutino decided to change the look. *Courtesy of Tom Cutino.*

1952 CHEVROLET FLEETLINE DELUXE

The last year the Chevrolet Fleetline Deluxe was produced was 1952. The fastback sloping of the roof adds a long streamline sweeping back. Tom acquired the car in Isleton when it was just a body and frame. He started by adding a Mustang 2 front suspension with disc brakes. The engine was a 283 small block attached to a Turbo 350 transmission powering the General Motors 12 Bolt rear end with disc brakes. The body came next; no problem for Tom, he does excellent body modifications. He installed custom-built headlights frenched in, as was the grille enclosure. The front bumper was flipped over and attached to an extended front pan. The hood was one piece with corners rounded and rain gutters removed. He then frenched in custom taillights and bumper. The two-piece windshield was refitted with a one-piece from a 1950 Oldsmobile. The paint job was a Pearl White with organic candy flames and green pin-striping. The car remains in Tom Cutino's personal collection and "runs and drives like a dream."

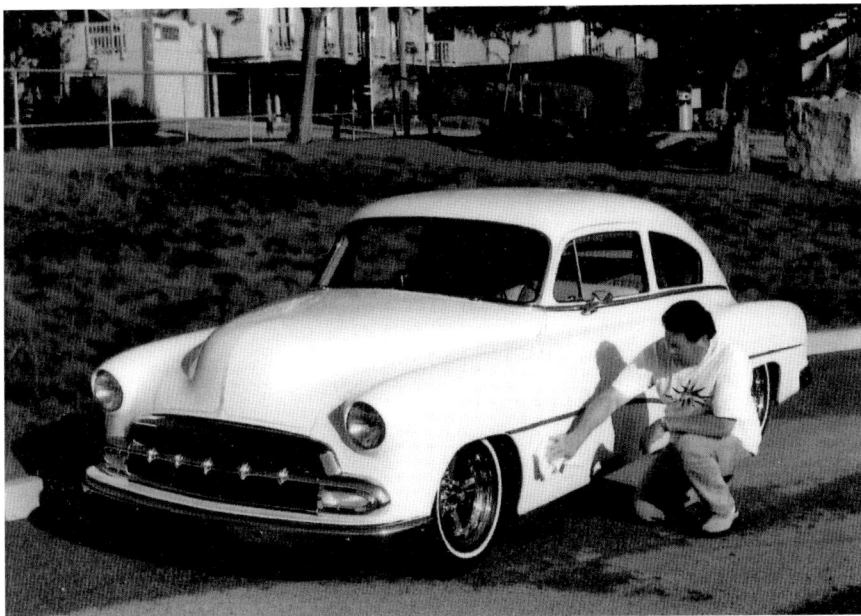

Tom Cutino proudly poses by his fine creation. *Courtesy of Tom Cutino.*

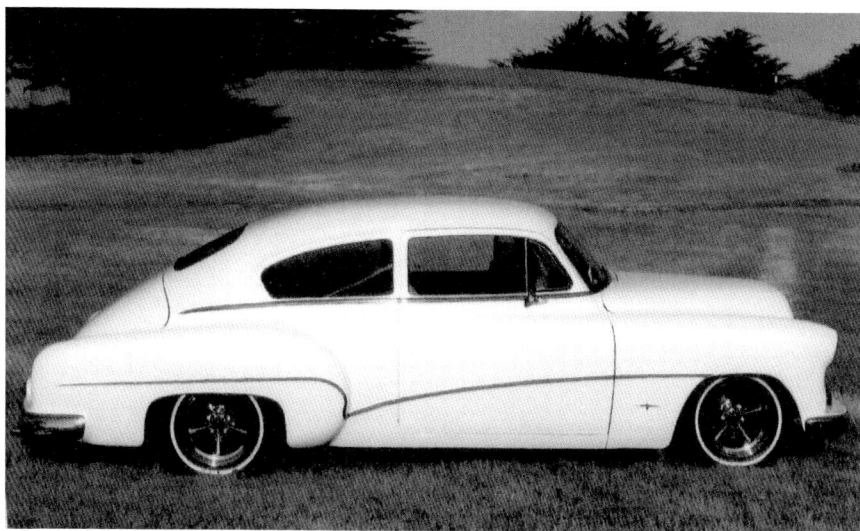

The side view of the '52 Chevy accentuates the sloping lines that fade backward from front to rear. The accent paint line follows the roof and truck shape to create lower flow lines. *Courtesy of Tom Cutino.*

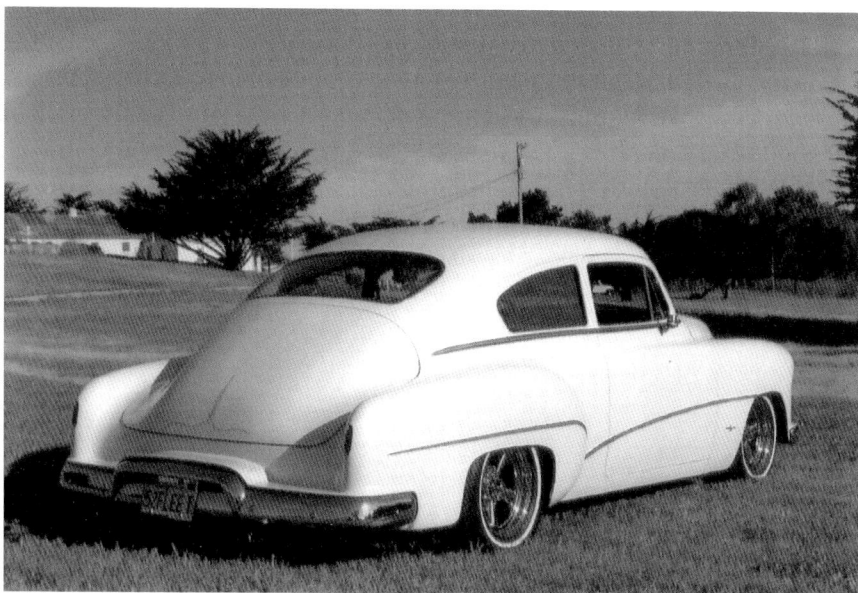

This back side view shows design genius that Tom captures. Everything is smooth, and the frenched taillights contribute to the total impact. *Courtesy of Tom Cutino.*

1953 CHEVROLET TWO-DOOR HARDTOP

This custom started out as your everyday transportation vehicle. It wasn't in the greatest shape when Tom purchased it in Carmel, California, from an older gentleman, who parted from it for fifty dollars. When Tom got the Chevy to his shop, he started customizing it immediately. He had been given a '65 Impala from one of his neighbors, and it was to be a parts donor to the '53. He pulled the stock engine and transmission and replaced them with the 283 engine and power-glide transmission. The next changes happened underneath. The suspension was modified and upgraded. Hydraulic lifts were installed. This way you could raise it up for driving and avoid the annoying tickets for being too low to the ground. That was accomplished by adjusting the suspension to the height of a pack of Lucky Strike cigarettes. That's an old way for measuring the ground clearance. If you could put the pack upright under the car, it was legal.

Tom moved on to customizing the body. The grille opening was hand-fabricated and molded in to fit the tube bar grille. Headlights were frenched

A 1953 Chevy two-door hardtop at the Grand National Roadster Show. This is another show winner that Tom Cutino built in his shop. *Courtesy of Tom Cutino.*

and hood corners rounded, and just behind the front wheel opening, he put '57 Buick teardrop portholes. In the back, the license plate was molded in along with '54 Chevy modified taillights. Tom chose a blended look for the paint job with Candy Pagan Gold blended to Candy Tangerine Orange micro flake. The interior was handmade by Tom and features an RCA 45 record player. Finishing off accessories, full-length drag pipes and Appleton spotlights were added.

1915 T ROADSTER PICKUP

A guy named Norm started building the roadster pickup but decided to sell it. Tom bought the roadster unfinished and began working on it at the same time Dennis Lesh was building his Track T. Dennis was able to help Tom with some fabrication work and teach him some special techniques he uses to this day. He still has the roadster and drives it regularly.

Tom Cutino finished this roadster with the help of Dennis Lesh. Tom and Dennis drove all over the place; they were doing local shows and just hanging out. *Courtesy of Tom Cutino.*

LUCKY SILVA

HOT RODS, MOTORCYCLES AND CUSTOM CARS

Lucky Silva is another very talented builder of custom cars and hot rods. He has lived just outside Isleton on the family ranch all his life.

Lucky has also been working on cars all his life. He's the one many would bring their cars to for some specialized work. Rod Dolk brought him his '34 Ford pickup for the beautiful blue paint job it still has. Lucky also worked on motorcycles, his 1971 Honda 750 being a perfect example. It was painted gold on the tank, frame and rear fender by hall-of-fame painter Art Himsl. It featured girder forks, which raise the front and extend the length of the bike. Along the way, Silva learned pointers from friends like Dale Kamen and his dad, Norman.

Lucky Silva also built some chopper-style motorcycles. This beauty sports extended girder front end forks and chrome everywhere. It was a '71 Honda 750 engine. *Courtesy of the Silva Collection.*

Ghost flames are so subtle, you might miss them. This is what design is all about. *Courtesy of the Silva Collection.*

Lucky also built a very nice '56 Chevy that was just right. It was two-toned blue and white and lowered, of course, with narrow whitewall tires and shiny mag wheels. On the lower panel between the front and rear wheel wells are subtle flames that strike the right balance. The Chevy is a perfect example of what you can accomplish with simple methods: color, chrome and stance.

The '32 Ford pickup is shown sitting beautifully by the Sacramento River with a gold body with black fenders. The truck has a chopped top; all bodywork was done by Dale and Danny Kamen. It was a winner at the Sacramento Autorama. Lucky has been working on it ever since, refining and refinishing the look and stance in his large barn-sized shop; he is another Delta car builder who does incredible work.

Lucky Silva's '32 Ford is at a favorite location along the Sacramento River. It is a mile wide there, but now the shoreline is covered with homes. It's a beautiful pickup with a fantastic background. *Courtesy of the Silva Collection.*

Lucky Silva's unfinished '32 pickup before it was painted. The photo was taken at his home just outside Isleton, California. *Courtesy of the Silva Collection.*

MANNY FERNANDEZ

1940 MERCURY

Sometimes, a story about a family treasure is told best by a family member. The car in question has a unique history. The following story is told by the amateur and professional. Both granted me permission to repeat them. Manny sent me a story based on his family's experiences.

(From a letter written by Manny Fernandez)

Butler Rugard had two custom cars built by Harry Westergard, one of them being the 1940 Mercury. When my dad Bill Fernandez got home from the Navy Seabee's after WW2 he bought the 1940 Mercury from Butler Rugard for $1,800 dollars. My dad used the Mercury as a hot rod until 1949 when he married his wife Pauline and it was used as a family car. The Mercury made many trips to L.A. over the Grapevine to see Pauline's folks.

In 1955 my dad traded in the Mercury at Walnut Grove at Wallace Ford Dealership for a 1955 Crown Victoria to some gentleman from Freeport who bought our 1940 Mercury. It wasn't long after that our family was going over to Galt to visit our Uncle Albert and on the side of the road along Highway 99 Freeway we spotted the Mercury broken down, with no one around. We left our phone number on the car; the Mercury was in pretty bad shape. The man called us back and Marie and I traded him a nice 1938 Chevrolet Coupe for the 1940 Mercury. We fixed up the Mercury really nice and used it going from Ryer Island up and down the river to Rio

Manny and Marie Fernandez's '40 Mercury in an orchard near their home. This was a family car with quite an impressive history, used for daily driving. *Courtesy of the Fernandez Collection.*

Vista High School for four years. We graduated, and I joined the USMC for four years, my sister stayed at home and used the Mercury to go back and forth to work from Ryer Island Sacramento at a Bank every day.

In January 1964 I got out of the service and Marie still used the Mercury up until she got married on November 28, 1964, she stored the Mercury where she lived until 1966 and asked if I wanted the Mercury back. So, I took the Mercury back in 1966 and stored it across the river at the Snell Ranch in a barn which Bill McCormick had bought, he let me store it until they tore the barn down in 1971.

So, I moved it back to Rio Vista at 101 California and Main streets where I lived even though I had no garage to park it in. Every time I would go away for the weekend or holiday with my wife I would get a ticket for not moving the Mercury on the street within 72 hours, this got old after a while and expensive. So, I decided to sell the Mercury, then my brother Randy said he wanted it, so I gave it to him. Randy didn't have it for long and he sold it to Bob Balsmier in Isleton. I don't know how long he kept the Mercury, but he sold it to a Ron Marguardi from Sacramento. My brother, sister and I looked for the car for a long time with no success. Then a bunch of us from Rio Vista used to go to the Carnival Cruise in Truckee in the 1990's each year. Arnold Gouveia, Thom Smith, Buddy Gann, Andy Crowe, Danny Brown, Jeff Fernandez, my brother, myself, Marie Delmugnaio, my sister and all their wife's and girlfriends. One year my brother Jeff and I were at the Carnival Cruise in Truckee with all the guys looking at hot rods when we spotted the old '40 Mercury. We talked with Ron Marguardi who owned the car, and we told our story about the Mercury's history. Jack Walker and Ed Gulley were partners on the project and Jack completed the purchase from Ron for the Mercury, where he said it had been stored for 30 years.

When I talked with Bob Balsmeier about his ownership of the car, he said he got it for $350. It was in pretty bad shape, with cracks in the top. It was now painted Oliver Tractor Green. No doubt the paint came from Dolk Tractor Company, which sold Oliver Tractors in Rio Vista. Bob lived in Isleton at that time and did some work on it in a barn. The split windshield was fogged up, so he got a new one and fixed that up. It ran a 265 flathead Chevy engine that he drove a lot—one time all the way up the mountains to Lake Tahoe, which is about 130 miles and a 6,200-foot climb. He lost first gear on the transmission and got along fine using second and third gears on the manual transmission. He sold the car without knowing how much it would be worth many years later. But he got a fair price for those days.

CUSTOM CARS MAGAZINE, AUGUST 1960

Letter to the Editor: Built by Dad…Owned by Daughter

Dear Sir:

I enjoy reading your magazine very much. I have enclosed some snapshots of my '40 Mercury. It was my dad's car and he and Harry Westergard did all the work on it. It's been chopped 4 inches and lowered. It has a jet-black paint job and has a white Carson top: on the inside of the top there is leopard fur. It has a chromed dash and door panel and the steering wheel is a Lincoln: it has leather upholstery. It has fade away fenders and push button doors.

It has a '40 Buick grille: the bumpers are Packard and Packard headlights are used. It has drag pipes and the taillights are Chevy units. The engine is a stock '40 Mercury. I am proud to be the girl that owns the best customized car in the area.
—Marie Fernandez
Walnut Grove, Calif.

You should be, Marie, your dad and his friend did a great job—Ed.

This vintage 1940 Mercury was shown at the prestigious Pebble Beach Concours d'Elegance in 2005 and the Sacramento Autorama in 2009. It was the feature car in a display area for the late Harry Westergard. There was a storyboard with pictures of cars he worked on along with a life-sized picture cutout of Harry and his wife. It was a great tribute to his contribution to the world of hot-rodding. It was purchased by a custom car collector who transported it to his home country of Greece, where it is now for sale with an estimated value of $140,000 (€100,000 or best serious offer). That's quite an increase in value for a car sold new off the showroom floor for $1,800.

WALT "WALDO" SCHMIT

1957 FORD FAIRLANE

The 1957 Ford Fairlane grew out of the Ford Motor Company's effort to replace Chevrolet as the top-selling car company. The result was a car with long flanks, tail fins and a lower profile. Ford was successful, and the Fairlane became the bestselling car in America. It has a somewhat square and wide body style, but very elegant. Walter Schmit had the nickname "Waldo," and his car was "The Cherry Bomb." Many show cars had nicknames: The Ala Kart, Golden Sahara, Beatnik Bandit and Kookies Car, to name a few of the famous ones. Waldo bought the Fairlane while he was a salesman at Bauman Motors, the local Ford dealership on Front Street, where the river runs behind the shop. The car started out as a beautiful two-door hardtop; anyone in the world could purchase one exactly like it in every detail down to the color of the carpet rugs. Waldo was a hot-rodder at heart, and hot-rodders don't leave anything alone for long. He was a member of the local car club, the Levee Lopers, with fellow guys who dug cars. Some of them liked customs and some racing, and most liked both. The club insisted all members drive safely and race on drag strips. Bauman Motors' body shop foreman Lenny Byer became a local legend fixing up cars. Jack Bauman, the owner, saw opportunity in the younger population who came in to have work done on their cars. They were car crazy, so he embraced them as current and future customers. After they were married and family men, they could buy their family cars from him. Waldo had earlier built a '49 Ford, and he used it in trade with Walt Rossini for the '57. Waldo and Lenny collaborated on the beginning changes to the car, nothing radical, just Candy Apple Red paint with gold scallops, pyramid moon hubcaps, wide whitewalls all around and drag pipes. He also displayed a Levee Lopers car club plaque on the back-window package shelf.

Waldo is pictured below with his arm proudly on the roof of the '57 when the customizing was in the early stages; there are gold scallops on the hood and above the rear tire side panel. But this was only the beginning—he had bigger plans ahead. In 1957, cars mostly had single headlights, so the customizing started with the addition of dual headlights. The stock headlight has a sort of bug-eyed look with high eyebrows, so quad headlights set in a new circled frame was a cooler look. That wasn't all; he inset the lights on a gold mesh screen set back inside. Then Lenny Byer molded an extreme peak over the top and ran a semicircle channel sweeping back twenty-four inches along the fender top with a cool antenna mounted inside, pointing to the front. It was leaded, sanded and primered. The engine hood had the corners rounded and under hood painted white.

Moving downward from the headlights, the stock grille was removed and a new one from a '54 Chevy, complete with clearance lights, was added. He added 1955 Pontiac bumpers to protect the front end. They added drag

A young Walt Schmit with his original '57 Ford he customized. It was later re-customized to give it a new makeover into a major car show winner. *Courtesy of the Schmit Collection.*

Walt kneels by his '57 at the high school view toward the river, a popular site. *Courtesy of the Schmit Collection.*

pipes that curved up into the body behind the front wheel well. The wheel wells' interiors were painted white, as was the entire undercarriage, and the Fairlane sported wide whitewall tires with 1959 Dodge Lancer hubcaps. The roof was not overlooked, and two distinctive square scoops were made. They were at the corners of the rear windows, about twenty-four inches long and six inches wide. The '57 Ford Fairlane came with long tail fins, which were a very popular feature on Detroit-style cars. Lenny took it a step further, extending the fins and bringing them to a very defined point. The taillight housing was a large teardrop shape. Inside the housing were two of the most popular taillights ever: rocket-shaped lenses side by side. Creatively, with smooth flow, two of these were placed inside the teardrop housing, held in place by a gold screen. They also removed the stock back bumper and smoothed everything out.

Lenny then applied the beautiful Candy Apple Red paint job for which he is remembered and famous. The finishing touch was painting white shading along the body lines. The interior was finished by Mac's Upholstery Shop of Isleton in a red-and-white theme. The dash was white tuck and roll Naugahyde synthetic leather, and seats were white with red tuck and roll

Oakland Roadster Show presentation of Walt Schmit and Lenny Byer's work turning the car into a complete new design and makeover. *Courtesy of the Marks Collection.*

The rear view of the Schmit car at the same show. It is completely opened up, hood, trunk and doors. The angel hair surrounding the car makes it looks like its floating on a cloud. *Courtesy of the Marks Collection.*

centers. It had a full red carpet on the floor. Door panels were white with red buttons. The trunk was also fully upholstered in red with white buttons. The modified 225-cubic-inch engine was finished with much chrome and the compartment finished in white.

The 1961 National Roadster Show was held on February 17–26 in the Oakland exhibition building. Waldo's entry was one of 125 custom cars and hot rods featured at the show.

The following article was printed in the *River News Herald* on March 1, 1961:

4 Vehicles Customized by Rio Vistan Win High Honors

Two autos, along with a Model A Ford Pickup and a motorcycle—all customized by Lenny Byers, of Rio Vista—walked off with top honors at the National Roadster Show just concluded after a 10-day run in Oakland. Byers, a Bauman Motors body shop employee, customized a 1957 Ford Fairlane 500, a 1947 Buick, the Model A Ford Pickup and the cycle.

More than 125 glamorous custom cars, fantastic hot rods, fabulous sports cars and new experimental models were exhibited during the competition which ended Sunday. In addition to competition on a national level, cars competed for the Western United States honors and California trophies. The 1957 Ford was exhibited by Walt Schmit, of Rio Vista. It took home the national prize, a giant trophy with plaque. The car is painted candy apple red with white trim. The interior is pleated upholstery in red and white.

The Ford Model A won the national prize in the roadster pickup division. Owned by Dave Dias, of Concord, the vehicle was trimmed in black and chrome. Carl Garcia, of Rio Vista, entered his customized motorcycle in competition with 18 others from throughout the United States. Garcia won the Western USA division trophy. The 1947 Buick owned and exhibited by Bob Palladino, of Brentwood, won the California competition in the custom hardtop division of the Oakland event. Palladino also received a trophy.

The following was announced in the *River News Herald* on March 8, 1961:

TOPS IN THE SHOW

This is a 1957 Ford a-la-Lenny Byers. The Bauman Motors body shop employee stands beside Walter Schmit's Ford which Byers [sic] customized for national competition. Judges at the National Roadster Show held recently in Oakland thought it was the best-looking customized car in the exhibit and they awarded it first place. A striking "candy apple red" finish accented with white and chrome, the vehicle even sports an upholstered trunk compartment. The upholstery, of course, is pleated red and white.

[This car disappeared forty years ago, and these pictures will refresh the memories of what the car looked like in its glory days. Waldo helped with the bodywork and Lenny's creativity made this the National Roadster show First Place Semi-Custom Show Winner.]

JACK COUGHLIN

1932 ROADSTER HIGHBOY

One of the most amazing hot rods you'll ever see of early home-built roadsters is Jack Coughlin's '32 Ford roadster. He was a mechanic by trade and built the car in his shop/garage at home. It's amazing that this roadster started out in Rio Vista and eventually made its way to be displayed at the Peterson Auto Muscum in Los Angeles.

John and Kirk Coughlin learned their mechanical skills from their dad. He had a talent for building hot rods, and the '28–'32 roadster was different. The first thing that is apparent is the uncommon stance. *Stance* in the car community means simply the way a car sits. The look of this hot rod sends a message: this is an aggressive car. It looks as if it is already in motion, a racehorse at the starting gate. Normally, '28–'32 Ford roadsters have full fenders that are outside the body. A Hi-Boy roadster has the fenders removed completely and has either no fenders or motorcycle fenders that are separate on each tire.

Coughlin's roadster was on display at the Peterson Museum, one of the world's largest automotive museums. The Peterson has over one hundred vehicles on display. That is half of the total collection; those not on display are stored in a basement vault. The 1932 roadster was sold at auction and now belongs to a private collection. The plaque on the display read:

31 Ford Hi Boy Roadster
This high boy is based on the body and custom hood. Its conversion took place when the original motor was replaced with a high compression

Left: Jack Coughlin was a mechanic by trade. His skill in building a hot rod from the ground up is remarkable. *Courtesy of the Coughlin Collection.*

Below: A 1932 Ford roadster, built by Jack Coughlin, in its award-winning glory. This Rio Vista car is displayed in a private collection by a very proud owner. *Courtesy of the Coughlin Collection.*

Down low, front view of the unique stance of Jack Coughlin's '32. Very popular look in those days. *Courtesy of the Coughlin Collection.*

On display is the Jack Coughlin roadster as it appeared in the Peterson Automotive Collect in Los Angeles, California. *Courtesy of the Coughlin Collection.*

Jack Coughlin's roadster at the Peterson Museum with a view of the chromed front suspension with display placard. *Courtesy of the Coughlin Collection.*

An open-door look at Jack Coughlin's '32 and the custom tuck and roll leather upholstery and cool interior. *Courtesy of the Coughlin Collection.*

Oldsmobile engine. The engine was an obvious choice because of its overhead value system provided horsepower that few flat-heads could match. The mid-century innovation to this car have remained untouched, making it a rare example of early hot rodding.

Jack created the exhaust pipes system throughout, from the manifold to rear exhaust pipes. The interior was hand-stitched at "A" Action Upholstery by Ken Foster. It is tan colored with pleats on the bench seat and door panels. Foster also handmade the dashboard.

It had a LaSalle transmission and Ford rear end with leaf spring suspension and brake drums. It rolled down the road on Kelsey Hays chrome wheels, hub caps and tires. Jack painted the car jet black, a typical color on early roadsters, and displayed his prize at the Sacramento Autorama show.

RON "BOOTS" HEATH

1932 FORD ROADSTER, WILDFIRE PICKUP, 1936 FORD

Ronald "Boots" Heath came to Rio Vista when he was thirteen years old and a freshman at Rio Vista High School. The family moved from Livingston, Montana, and his dad got a job working at C.P.C. Farms on nearby Hasting Island. Boots began working on cars when he was twelve years old and learned mostly on his own.

His first hot rod was a 1932 Ford coupe. It was hopped up, painted white with flames. After high school and his marriage to Judy, he got a job working for one of the Delta's talented car customizers, Dale "Slim" Kamen. They worked together at Dunn and Sons in Isleton. During the eight years Heath worked with Dale, he learned painting, body and fender repair and the now lost art of using lead for custom work. After that, he was employed at Dolk Tractor, where he worked on tractors and the owner's son Rod's '34 Ford pickup. Boots unfortunately contracted lead poisoning and decided to change occupations. He told me that after work, the boys would sit out back and have a cold beer. Well, he didn't drink beer, and according to him, that's why he got the lead poisoning and the beer boys didn't—the beer. Now that could be a tall tale, but it sounds like a reasonable story, who knows? Ron was always interested in real estate and moved to Lodi, where he got a job at Aladdin Real Estate, where he worked for three years. He became a broker and started a partnership, Ferrero and Heath Real Estate, and was in the real estate business for thirty years. During this time, he continued to work in his home garage on custom cars and trucks.

Boots Heath's '32 roadster was his first. Pictured here by the city park with vintage flames popular in the '50s. *Courtesy of the Heath Collection.*

Big trophies for big car shows. Boots Heath is pictured here with awards won by being the best at what he does. *Courtesy of Heath Collection.*

They are called suicide doors because it was conceivably dangerous to open doors into traffic. It is a really cool way to be different yet easier to enter and exit the truck. *Courtesy of the Heath Collection.*

One of the trucks he built was a 1956 Ford F-100. The truck won many awards and underwent changes too numerous to mention, but I'll try: The entire chassis and suspension were changed and updated. The body also completely changed—the roof and cab were cut off and removed.

Boots changed conventional opening doors to suicide style, where they opened for a forward exit, and added a new convertible top, handmade and completely removable. The truck bed was cut off and a 1956 Studebaker pickup bed and fenders custom fabricated to fit. It was featured in the February 2002 issue of *Street Trucks* magazine in a four-page article, with nine color pictures and an in-depth story of the construction. After rolling out of the garage, it won at the Sacramento Autorama as "Most Outstanding Truck of Show." Ron Heath also won at the Rio Vista Bass Derby car show "Best of Show." At Santa Maria, he won "F-100 top Five" out of five hundred entries. In Reno, at Horizon Car Show it won "Best of Show." It was named "Wildfire."

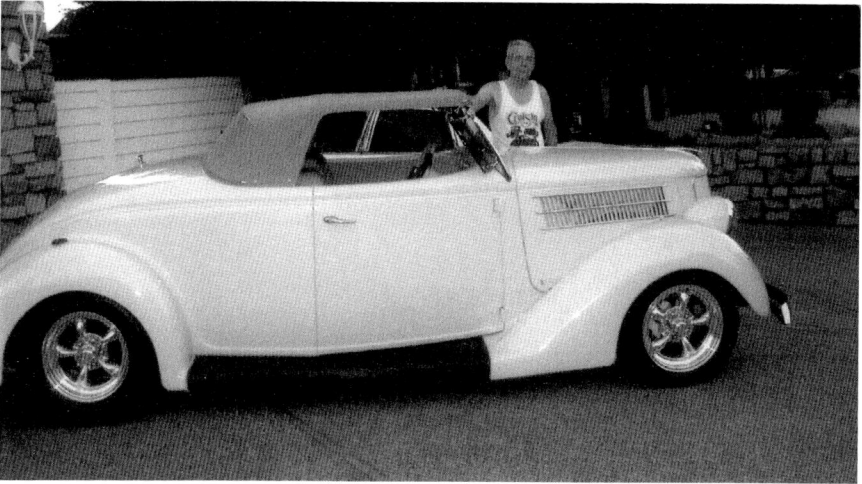

Boots Heath by his '36 Ford roadster. He bought it from an online catalogue sight unseen and shipped from a southern state. It turned out to be in bad shape, but that was a minor challenge for him. *Courtesy of the Heath Collection.*

Boots Heath's open door and hood on his '36 Ford show what quality is all about. Everything is new and clean and show ready. *Courtesy of the Heath Collection.*

His next project was a 1936 Ford roadster, a car he had been looking for for ten years. He ordered it off the internet based on the pictures and description, and it was in worse condition than described. He rebuilt the car from the ground up.

The interior was beautifully finished in white and brown leather and boasts a yellow dash and all new gauges and electronics. It turned out to be another outstanding custom car completed by Ron "Boots" Heath.

DAVE DIAS

1928 FORD ROADSTER PICKUP

Rod & Custom magazine had a nice article in August 1960 titled "Fast Freight." In the accompanying picture is Lenny Byer, leaning on the windshield of the pickup, talking to Dave. Both wear big smiles and seem to be enjoying themselves. Dave and Lenny were best friends. I guess it's the epitome of compliments when your dream car appears on the cover of a hot rod magazine. This is an example of an old school build. Dave, a sheet metal journeyman by trade, did all sheet metal work on the car, and his knowledge of welding was essential for completing the truck. It's another example of a Frankenstein collection of parts from other vehicles making a new one. So how did this truck begin?

The original truck looked like a vehicle used for work. It had been put to work in the fields hauling whatever needed hauling. Dave acquired it from his father-in-law around 1950. The appearance was actually deceiving; it ran well and was his everyday transportation. It was functional, but to make it into a custom show car, every square inch needed repair, sandblasting, derusting and a good scrub-down.

In the book *Lost Hot Rods II*, author Pat Ganahl wrote about Dave's truck:

> Dave Dias of Concord, California, went a little further than most in reshaping his 1928. First, he Z-cut and kicked up the rear of the 1928 frame 5 ½ inches to get the rear to sit low. Then he moved the body back about 6 inches to make room for the big 1949 Cadillac V-8 he punched out to 342 ci. Being a sheet-metal worker, he then made a longer three-piece,

FAST FREIGHT

cad-powered pickup has short bed, but hauls!

The quaint appearance of the '28-'29 Ford roadster pickup — long a favorite of R&C's Editors — has been brought to an apex in Dave Dias' black track. "A-bone" enthusiasts will quickly note that the fenders are not stock for the year of the bucket, but are the more sweeping '31 models — a subtle but enhancing swap. Distinctive wheels are sans caps, showing construction with 15" hoops mounted on '38 Ford centers, a weight-saving and strength gaining design with the mounting lugs near the outer perimeter of the drum. Nuts are chromed.

photos by George Barnley

ROD & CUSTOM • AUGUST, 1960

24

Lenny Byer (*left*) and Dave Dias admiring his Ford roadster pickup, built by Dave and finished by Lenny. *From* Rod & Custom, *August 1960.*

louvered hood. And behind the body he shortened the pickup bed to a mere 3 feet. Finally, he added sleeker 1931 fenders, bobbing the rears several inches to match the bed, and adding a sheet-metal apron between them. With the A wind-shield chopped a healthy and a short-chromed roll bar just peeking above the back of the cab, this all combined to give this black roadster pickup a look somewhere between a 1940s sports car and a dirt track racer. Dias' choice of wide-5, 1939 Ford wheels, as well as white upholstery rolled over the cab's edges, added to the track roadster image.

Dave told me about the wheels. He was particularly proud of them, as they were original, but he kept the centers and welded them to fifteen-inch rims, painted them and added chrome nuts and new tip. When it came time to do the finishing touches, Dave turned to his very good friend Lenny Byer. They had served together in the U.S. Army in Salzburg, Austria. Lenny did all the finishing body work and painted the pickup in Rio Vista. They finished it up with top and interior upholstery stitched in Concord by Jim Carroll. The roll bar was solidly secured for another reason. Dave fabricated a car seat for his young son, with room for his wife. When it came time for the paint job, he chose black. It was first painted black by Lenny.

Dave drove it for a while to test the paint and double-check for any imperfections. A black paint job is one of the most difficult to do because most blemishes are barely detectable. They checked and checked again all surfaces and then sanded it down, primered it and finally laid down a perfect paint job. Just about every part that they could remove was chrome plated, including the firewall, engine parts and radiator. Dave related to me the story of the pin-striping on the pickup. He said he had been trying for some time to get it striped and wanted the best to do it. That would be "Tommy the Greek," a legend in the custom car culture world. When Dave cornered Tommy at the Oakland National Car Show for a commitment to do it, he said, "Let's do it right now." Tommy got his kit together and proceeded to do the entire car right on the showroom floor. This was an unusual occurrence and delighted the crowd. The entire job was observed by the many hundreds in attendance. On the way to another car show, they had trouble, as the truck was secured to a trailer and covered with a tarp. If you've ever done that, then you know what happens when the wind blows around the tarp—it rubs on the paint. It did, and the tops of the fenders had some damage. Luckily, Lenny was

Dave Dias drove this truck long before he customized it. It ran very well. *Courtesy of Dave Dias.*

This is the finished roadster pickup by Lenny Byer and Dave Dias. *Courtesy of Dave Dias.*

along and said don't worry; he promptly rubbed out the fender tops, and they were good as new.

Pictured here is the finished roadster, a show winner in every contest in which it competed. So where is it today? It resides in the private collection of John Mumford in South San Francisco, California. There are a few minor changes, but it is as beautiful now as when Dave last owned it. Dave really likes the restoration, except the wheels. His were truly original. Occasionally, John opens his museum to the public to see his collection—maybe we'll see it one day.

DALE "SLIM" KAMEN

AMERICA'S MOST BEAUTIFUL ROADSTER

Dale's nickname was "Slim," and it fit him well. He stood six feet, six inches tall and was thin at that. He was a master craftsman who performed lots of normal bodywork that dealers take in on a regular basis. He became an expert at dolly and hammer work and lead, which is difficult to work with and perfect. He perfected that medium and passed on his experience to his son Danny and other eager body men in training.

He is pictured in one of the most famous roadsters in the American automobile history: the 1951 America's Most Beautiful Roadster. Slim worked alongside Harry Westergard, who is remembered as a pioneer of

This vintage photo has Dale "Slim" Kamen sitting in the car he helped create. This was work in progress for the roadster that would win the Oakland National Car Show in 1952. *Courtesy of Danny Kamen.*

sheet metal customizing. They both worked at a Studebaker dealership for Rico Squalia, who hand-built most of the AMBR award winner. Dale worked beside Harry on the grille, belly pan and the turtleback parts of the car and did the prep work and shot the Matador Red paint job. Later, when the dealership changed hands to become Dunn and Sons, the owner built a brand-new paint booth for Dale to do his paint work.

In the 1970s, he relocated to his own body shop business in Walnut Grove: Delta Body Works. This is where he taught his son Danny to do body and paint work and especially how to work with lead. Dale did work on numerous custom cars, including Lucky Silva's '32 Ford chopped-top pickup truck; Doug Schafer's '32 Ford; Robby Weber's '41 Ford delivery; Art and Nini Fevereiro's '55 Chevys; Carl Dolk's '32 Ford sedan; Bobby Hadden's '50 Ford sedan, August Correia's '29 Ford roadster; and Rod Dolk's '34 Ford pickup. Most of these cars are pictured in this book.

PART II

THE CARS

HARRY HANSEN

1952 CHEVROLET HARDTOP

One of the coolest customs that came out of Rio Vista and the Sacramento Delta during the '50s and '60s was a 1952 Chevy Bel Air hardtop from a local automobile dealer, Abel Chevrolet. It was factory stock, built by Detroit to be a nice family car. Harry had plans to make a cool custom, and the changes he made were incredible. Harry is a rancher who still lives near Birds Landing in the rich Montezuma Hills. Back then, it was grazing land for sheep and multiple natural gas wells, and today, gigantic windmills 750 strong surround his property, which has a great view of Mount Diablo. Hansen was another teenager who wanted to be part of the hot rod craze, and he contacted Lenny Byer, body shop manager at Bauman Motors, the Ford dealership. They began planning a complete remodel of the vehicle with longer body lines dropped four inches lower by cutting the coil springs.

The first thing to do when customizing a car is remove all chrome, including hood ornaments, door handles, antennas, trunk emblems and body trim. Then the Bel Air was sanded and seams filled with lead and sanded more. That finished the work, and everything was primered over. There were few cars in that era without primer spots—it was a mark of pride for the ongoing work being done. The grill and bumper were removed, and the job of transforming the front end began. Lenny mounted and molded in the chrome grille shell from a '55 Chevy and put a '58 Ford mesh screen to fill the hole. Mounted onto the mesh screen was the center grille piece from a '57 Corvette. The thirteen mounted teeth floating on the gold mesh

This is an early semi-custom multi-award winner. This '52 Chevrolet is a classic in design and performance. The design both inside and outside are outstanding; the powerhouse full-blown Corvette engine is amazing. *Courtesy of Harry Hansen.*

screen gave it a daunting look. All seams were lead filled, and a rounded peak was formed to run the length of the hood and downward at the nose of the hood. Along the sides of the hood were two handmade scoops, and two radio aerials projected outward from there. The headlights were from a '53 Mercury, set back and frenched in for a bold look. The fender is extended over the headlights for a hooded effect. The front bumper, as it turned out, was perfect, arched in a single smooth wraparound. The two-piece split windshield was replaced with a '52 Oldsmobile single-piece glass windshield. This was a popular added feature.

On the back of the roof, a custom-made scoop was added. This mimicked the '58 Chevy that had a one-piece chrome molding. Lenny's scoop used his special feature: five chrome balls mounted inside the opening for a unique, one-of-a-kind look. The two chrome strip moldings running down the length were retained since they fit the look, but other parts didn't and were removed. The door handles were removed, and push-button openers were placed under the door on the frame. The stock rear fender skirts were kept but customized with a flare molding. The rear portion got the full Byer's treatment. On the factory car, the designers brought the fenders down and rounded. This is where Lenny Byer really disagreed with Detroit. He brought the fenders straight out thirteen inches at Harry's insistence. In addition,

'56 Packard taillight units—complete with white backup lens—were set below the arrowhead-shaped fins. Another dynamic look at the rear is the '56 Chevy bumper. It fits as if it were designed to be there. Turning to the engine compartment, Harry chose a brand-new crate Corvette engine from dealer Abel Chevrolet. As if that wasn't powerful enough, he had Tommy Bettencourt add on a McCullough supercharger.

Moving inside that passenger compartment, Harry Hansen had Mack McNeil of Mac's Custom Interiors in Isleton do the stitching. Mac's was known for beautiful interior work, and Harry's '52 is a perfect example of it. The seats are tuck and roll white Naugahyde and candy red nylon frieze carpets. The headliner was white Naugahyde and the trunk fully finished in the same colors. Harry added another unusual feature: a custom-made and fitted engine cover in the same color theme. Full-length drag pipes and Appleton spotlights completed the accessories. The final part of the project was custom paint. As noted earlier, Lenny Byer was known for his Candy Apple Red lacquer paint jobs. Finally, Harry brought in a pin-striper from Oakland. The artist was known only as "The Firehouse Striper," and he added the fine lines. Broad whitewall tires and '56 Olds spinner hubcaps completed the package, and it was done. The car was a show winner in the Sacramento Autorama and Fresno Autorama, and at the Twelfth Annual Roadster show, his entry placard read:

> *HARRY HANSEN of Rio Vista, 1952 Chevrolet Bel Air. Frenched Packard taillights and headlights. '57 Chevrolet shell, '57 Corvette grille, '58 Ford mesh, Impala air scoop. Radio aerials scooped adjacent to the hood and headlights. Car lowered four-inches. Exterior is painted Candy Apple and striped by Firehouse striper. Interior is tucked and rolled white naugahyde and candy apple nylon frieze. Upholstery by Mack's Upholstery in Isleton Calif.*
>
> *Body work and paint done by Byer's Custom Painting, Bauman Motors, Rio Vista.*

Harry's splendid custom car won the first-place semi-custom award.

BOBBY HADDEN

1950 FORD COUPE

Bobby Hadden had to make a decision. He was a sophomore at Rio Vista High School, and he had to choose a car. The choice was between two used cars: a 1956 Plymouth with a six-cylinder engine or a 1950 Ford with a flathead V-8 motor. They were both for sale at the Ford dealership, and the money he made working for his dad as an apprentice was burning a hole in his pocket. His situation was unique because he was only fifteen and a half years old. Bobby said it wasn't much of a choice because the Ford ruled the road. Bobby picked the Ford with the big engine. The 1950 Ford is known by the nickname "The Shoebox Ford." It is a slab-sided, "pontoon" style that was defined as "all-enveloping bodywork, straight-through side styling, slab styling." The engine was a 239-cubic-inch flathead V-8 with one hundred horsepower. So why is it nicknamed a flathead engine? In technical terms, it means that the cylinder heads are flat as a pancake—that's why.

Bobby wanted to begin customizing it right away, so he talked with the best body man around: Lenny Byer, who was the body shop manager right there where Hadden bought the car: Bauman Motors in Rio Vista. Few teenagers left their cars in stock condition, and Bobby said they got together and talked about what custom features they would do. The first thing that was usually done was remove the hood and truck emblems, so that's what he did. Then Lenny put forward a design he did that resembled a 1958 Chevy Impala rear roof scoop. He then mounted five chrome ball bearings inside the opening. The body was prepared for a custom paint job—Tahitian Red lacquer was the choice—and spray painted in the paint booth. It was then buffed out and

The side view of Satan, the so-nicknamed ride of Bobby Hadden. It is a mild car with subtle yet effective styling that caught the girls' eyes, he tells me. *Courtesy of Bobby Hadden.*

polished to a brilliant shine. Bobby's artist friend Glen Abrescy convinced him his car needed a proper name, so it became "Satan." Glen used gold leaf to create the slanted lettering on the panel just behind the front wheel wells and finished it off with pin-striping.

Next was the addition of a set of Appleton spotlights mounted facing down. Then hubcaps were added: Oldsmobile 1956 Fiesta spinners (the most stolen hubcaps in history). Bobby worked and saved until he could afford (with his parents pitching in) to do the interior. The best shop around was just down the road in Isleton. Mac's Upholstery was the choice of many hot-rodders who wanted tuck and roll upholstery. Naugahyde is the material most used, for it is easily cleaned and durable artificial leather. He chose red and white seats with red carpets and a white headliner. Every custom car is lowered to increase the profile and look cool. That was accomplished with cut and welded springs, U-bolts and wood blocks: two-inch front, three-and-a-half-inch rear brought it to the desired stance and occasional fix-it ticket. He hopped up the engine with three Stromberg 97 carburetors with a Mallory ignition and dual exhausts with chromed tips. He bought all the interior chrome from a similar car that had an accident and installed the pieces. Bobby showed the car at area car shows and raced it at nearby Kingdon Drag Strip. It was there he stripped all the gears.

BILL CABRAL

1954 FORD/1958 OLDSMOBILE

Bill Cabral customized a 1954 Ford that turned out to be a real head turner. There are a couple of things he did that really made it really cool. It was lowered and drag pipes added to smooth out the stance. It starts with all that chrome car makers in the '50s seemed to put everywhere. Customizers use minimal manufacturer's chrome, so off most of it went. In front, the emblems were removed as well as the bumper guards. The square hood corners were rounded and Appleton spotlights mounted. The grille was stock with the bullet centerpiece removed. The tires were wide whitewalls with classic Fiesta spinner hubcaps. Rico Squalia hopped up the engine. It was topped off with a Lenny Byer custom Goldenrod Yellow paint job.

You don't see many 1958 Oldsmobiles around anymore, but Bill Cabal's was the best one of any we've seen around here. It was another fine custom by Lenny Byer at Bauman Motors body shop. Talk about a low profile—it had an air lift system, and every time Bill parked, it slowly sank to the ground. It was customized with many features of the day, including Appleton spotlights by the windshield and long drag pipes from front to rear wheel wells. There were other uncommon additions like scooped rear fenders and the aforementioned drag pipes—these were molded in a short housing, as they exited the manifold pipes. A semicircle scoop with an antenna facing forward ran along the front fenders behind the headlights.

When the body work was finished and seventeen coats of Metallic Kelly-Green lacquer were sprayed on, what a sight it was coming down the drag on

Above: Bill Cabral's very smooth, mild, semi-custom 1954 Ford is how cool a car can look with careful planning to make it look that way. Again, Lenny Byer's custom work is flawless. *Courtesy of the Cabral Collection.*

Right: The Bill Cabral '58 Oldsmobile is seen on display in Rio Vista at Bauman Motors car show. The beautiful Byer's Metallic Green paint job is highlighted. *Courtesy of the Cabral Collection.*

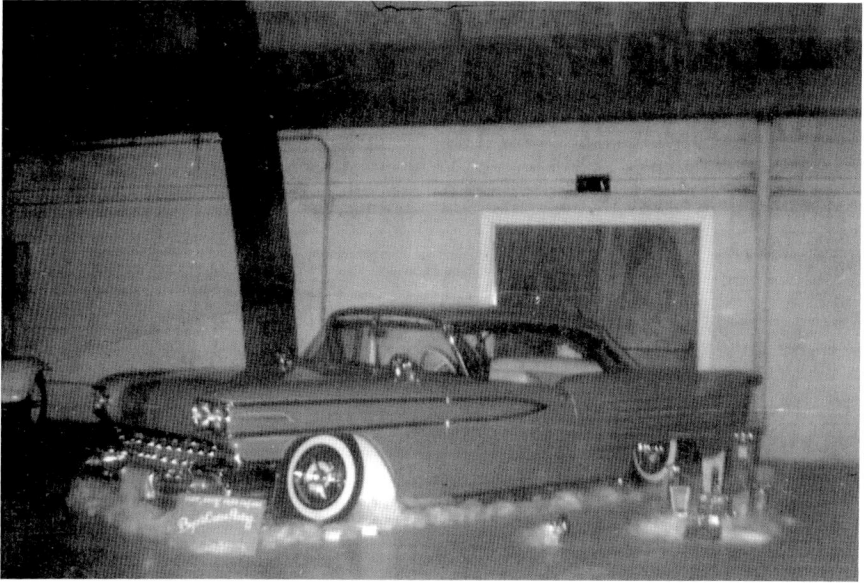

Bill Cabral's '58 Oldsmobile displayed at 1960 Lodi Road Angles Customcade car show in Lodi, California. Trophies are from the Rio Vista Levee Lopers. *Courtesy of the Cabral Collection.*

Main Street in Rio Vista. The hubcaps were from a '56 Dodge Lancer with four bar spinners brightly flashing the light with each turn of the whitewall tires. It sat so low you'd wonder how it ever managed to go over a hump in the road without bottoming out. The car was brilliant in color and chrome.

Bill entered it in a Lodi Car Show, and here is the listing from the original program:

> *Road Angles Inc. presents: CUSTOMCADE*
> *Car Show in Lodi, Ca.*
> *May 15, 1959*
> *From the official program:*
> *Semi-Custom Sedan*
> *Series 250*
> *#252 Bill Cabral—Rio Vista—Levee Lopers*
> *1958 Oldsmobile painted 17 coats light green. Rear fender scooped, drag pipes flared body. Front fender antennas dished and scooped.*

The car finished second place in the show.

WAYNE CULP

1950 MERCURY

Was Wayne's '50 Merc truly a lead sled? This is an interesting question because the term is generic in nature but actually has definite body modifications that qualify it. Wayne Culp's Mercury qualifies because it features frenching, emblem removal, trim removal, drip rail removal, door handle and lock removal and grill modifications. He did not chop or channel it. These Mercs have a solid, heavy look and weigh in at 3,500 pounds, nearly two tons. Hollywood loves the car, and directors have cast it in numerous movies. The car (lead sled) is sometimes cast as a heavy, sometimes good, but more often the bad guys' vehicle. In *Rebel Without a Cause*, James Dean drives a 1949 Merc Coupe; in *Cobra*, Sylvester Stallone is behind the wheel of a 1950 Merc; and in *American Graffiti*, the Pharaohs cruise in a chopped 1951 coupe.

Wayne's Merc is classified as a 1950 Mercury two-door, six-passenger coupe (a car with a fixed roof and two doors). It is a beautiful car with what Detroit called the "pontoon" look, where running boards were eliminated and the body side ran smooth from front to rear. Wayne, like most kids his age, wanted to be part of the hot rod craze sweeping the nation. There was, at that time, a drive-in restaurant at the Virginia Drive intersection coming west into Rio Vista off the bridge. It was there that Wayne got a job at Hamburger Haven while he was in high school. He started saving money to buy a car and fix it up. He found a 1950 Mercury and was able to buy it for $300, not bad for a fifteen-year-old young man. Like most of his car buddies, he went to Bauman Motors Ford dealership to talk with Lenny

The front of the Culp '50 Merc coming at you must have been a sight to see in the day. The low profile with a shark-like open jaws was an awesome look. *Courtesy of the Culp Collection.*

Byer, the body shop foreman. A teenager would have to do the customizing as he could afford it. It was how most cars were customized, one thing at a time, with it being in primer paint most of the time. Lead was used as a filler when forming and smoothing a car's metal surface. It is a difficult procedure to master, and the team at Bauman's body shop were experts.

Wayne had the hood done first; the seam down the middle was welded together, leaded, and sanded. Lenny crafted a peak that extended from the back down and over the nose. Not stopping there, the hood corners were rounded, and midway down the side of the hood edge, a scoop was formed. This was another one of Lenny's subtle touches. The grille opening was

The back view of Wayne Culp's Merc is powerful, like the front. Low is the word here, with lake pipes adding to that look. The canted taillights pull your eyes to the molded raised-crease down the trunk. *Courtesy of the Culp Collection.*

next. It was a shaped and molded opening made to fit the '54 Chevy grill with nine teeth. The front headlights were next and both frenched very nicely, to blend into the look. The side of the car maintained the smooth look with a single chrome strip extending from the front wheel wells to the taillights. Also added were drag pipes from front wheel well to rear wheel well; this visual effect makes your eyes follow the long length of the car front to rear in one continuous motion.

If you happened to pull up behind Wayne's car at a stoplight, you would immediately notice the taillights. They were bright red lights at an odd angle—*canted* we called it, pointed outward.

EDWARD "TIPPEE" DEL CHARO

1960 OLDSMOBILE

This clean, mild, custom '60 Oldsmobile hardtop is very long and wide. It has the necessary styling changes that make it a custom. The beautiful Metallic Burgundy paint job was done by Lenny Byer's shop. It looks great, with lots of chrome molding and Appleton spotlights. The chrome reversed rims are framed with fat whitewalls and painted white inter-walls. What sets it apart is a full white with red stripes Naugahyde tuck and rolled interior. The doors, seats and dashboard made this Olds a smooth ride for cruising.

Tippee Del Charo's 1960 Oldsmobile smooth cruiser at the Bauman Motors car show in Rio Vista, California. *Courtesy of the Del Charo Collection.*

RON DEBASCO

1955 CHEVROLET

Ron's '55 Chevy is another example of a very mild custom. There were many styles like his; the idea was to have a cool car on a tight budget. There are several requirements to get to the proper look. The first and most noticeable was lowering the car, and that was done by cutting coils out of the springs and welding them back together. Another method was using clamps to tighten the coils together.

Adding full-length lake-style pipes from the front wheel well to the rear wheel well enhanced the perception that the car was lower than it

Ron DaBasco's 1955 Chevy two-door hardtop cruiser was very mild. It was his everyday transportation with the right touches to make it his part of the custom car craze. *Courtesy of Ron DeBasco.*

actually was. These elements gave Ron's Chevy the nice stance it has. The next accessory would be the Appleton spotlights on each side of the front window. They were dummy nonworking lights that added the right look in a canted position. The premier style of wheels and tires in those days were wide whitewall tires and custom hub caps pyramid style, with three blades each.

ROD DOLK

1934 FORD PICKUP

June 5, 1959, was graduation day for the eighth-grade class of Rio Vista Riverview Elementary School. Rod Dolk's father, Stan, gave him what was to become a lifelong project when he was only fourteen years old. He had traded an old plow from the family tractor business for an abandoned 1934 Ford pickup from the Light Ranch on Ryer Island.

They brought it into the tractor shop and found many parts of the truck missing. This vehicle would not be repaired to be a shop truck—it was to be a hot rod. Transforming the pickup into a hot rod meant that major bodywork was necessary. Sectioning would be the first major change; the entire profile would be lowered to a more streamlined look. It is a major job, since it requires that the entire body be cut in half lengthwise. Careful calculations were necessary to be sure it would fit back together correctly three inches narrower. Sectioning is one of the most difficult bodywork jobs to do. Other body parts were also cut down including the bed and grille. The bed was also shortened, and when it was put back together on the frame, adjustments were necessary. When the car was lowered, they tinkered until the fit and look were correct. Wheels and tires were installed, and a flathead V-8 engine mounted into place. Lucky Silva applied the blue paint job.

They got the truck running about the time Rod got his driver's license at sixteen. His high school graduation present was a 283 Chevy engine from a friend of his dad's wrecking yard in Salinas. Rod went on to Sacramento State College, got a draft notice and married Vicki. He served his two-year

Rod Dolk's vintage '34 Ford pickup without hood side panels and big, wide, whitewall tires, with baby moon hubcaps. This is the very beginning. *Courtesy of Rod Dolk.*

Rod's pickup and his brother's '32 Ford Sedan in an antique photo in front of their home. *Courtesy of Rod Dolk.*

Nice side profile of the Rod Dolk pickup with a view of the Model A body lines. *Courtesy of Rod Dolk.*

The front of Rod Dolk's '34 Ford pickup out for a photo opportunity and just driving around taking pictures. *Courtesy of Rod Dolk.*

enlistment in the U.S. Army, finished college and returned to the family business his grandfather started in Rio Vista: Dolk Tractor Service. He continued working on the '34 and did a three-inch top chop. Many area car people have helped Rod with the truck, including "Boots" Heath, Dale "Slim" Kamen and Lucky Silva, to name a few. Today, it is a fine-looking truck, still driving around the area and at local car shows. It's amazing that it is still a family possession with around 160,000 miles.

Bill Cabral's very smooth, mild, semi-custom 1954 Ford is how cool a car can look with careful planning to make it look that way. Again, Lenny Byer's custom work is flawless. *Courtesy of the Cabral Collection.*

Wally Marks poses with his '55 Chevy. The style changes are not easily noticed because they blend in. Sometimes, simplicity brings out the best in a car. *Courtesy of Norman Marks.*

Above: The nose of Jack's Deuce shows the nice reflection of the Regency Purple paint. *Courtesy of the Schafer Collection*.

Left: The taillights on Jim's '51 are Packard are one of the most popular features used on a custom car. The retro flair and style are still super cool. *Courtesy of Jim Morris*.

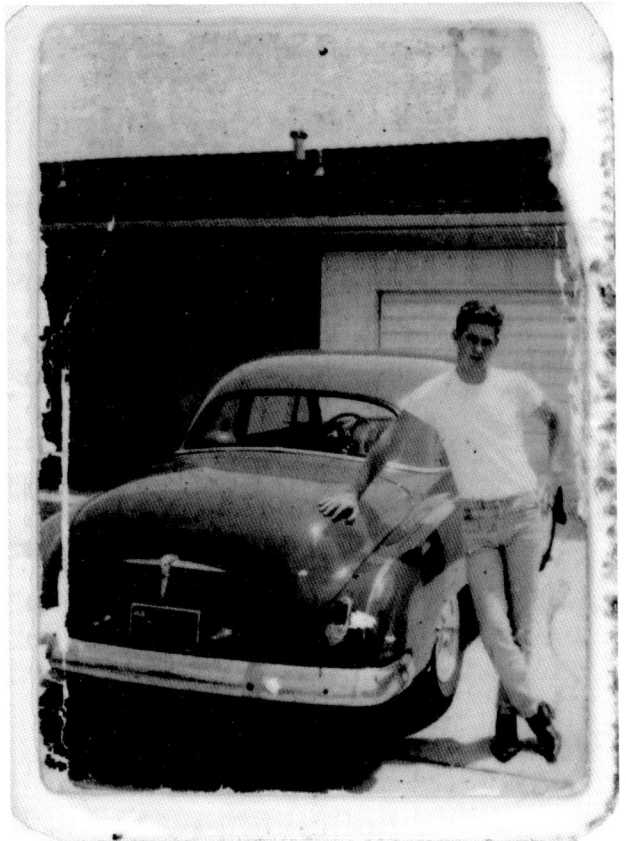

Top: This is a father teaching his son the mechanics of automotive building. They are at their home garage working together. *Courtesy of the Coughlin Collection.*

Right: Author with his 1950 Chevrolet, two-door hard-top Chevy painted 1965 Mustang Orange, circa 1965. *Callahan Collection.*

Tom Cutino finished this roadster with the help of Dennis Lesh. Tom and Dennis drove all over the place; they were doing local shows and just hanging out. *Courtesy of Tom Cutino Collection.*

This is the same '52 gold Ford after Tom Cutino decided to change the look. *Courtesy of Tom Cutino.*

Al and Jane Thurman's 1931 Ford Roadster beginning its transformation to show quality. *Courtesy of the Thurman Collection.*

Al Thurman stands proudly by his completed restoration; it means so much to the family. *Courtesy of the Thurman Collection.*

Rod's pickup and his brother's '32 Ford Sedan in an antique photo in front of their home. *Courtesy of Rod Dolk.*

Twig Silva's panel really catches your eye with its bright yellow paint, shiny brass fittings and gold leaf lettering. It would be hard to miss this one on the drag. *Courtesy of the Silva Collection.*

Down low, front view of the unique stance of Jack Coughlin's '32. Very popular look in those days. *Courtesy of the Coughlin Collection.*

Lucky Silva's '32 pickup along the mile-wide Sacramento River on a vacant lot. Nice setting on a nice day. *Courtesy of Lucky Silva.*

Top: Ghost flames are so subtle, you might miss them. This is what design is all about. *Courtesy of the Silva Collection.*

Left: Lucky Silva '32 primered and looking good. Lowered to the ground and prepped to be painted. *Courtesy of Lucky Silva.*

Lucky Silva also built some chopper-style motorcycles. This beauty sports extended girder front end forks and chrome everywhere. It was a '71 Honda 750 engine. *Courtesy of the Silva Collection.*

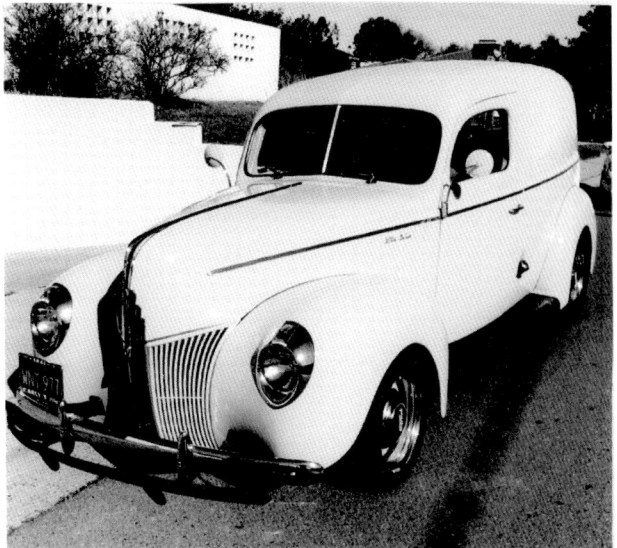

Robbie Weber's '41 Ford Sedan Delivery is looking extremely good on a bright sunny day, accentuating the flawless bright-yellow paint job. *Callahan Collection.*

Ernie Lucas shows his teenage dreams of racing became a reality with his Polara on a drag strip. *Courtesy of Ernie Lucas.*

Dennis Lesh sits on Tom Cutino's street roadster pickup at a Goodguys car show in Pleasanton, California. *Courtesy of the Lesh Collection.*

An in-process shot of the Dennis Lesh '28 roadster. It has a different engine and hood that were changed when finished. *Courtesy of the Lesh Collection.*

A view from above of the shop, nothing fancy, but laid out and maintained in proper order. Unlike many other shops' appearance, this is clean and orderly. *Courtesy of the Lesh Collection.*

Randy Fernandez was a fan of flames—not the big ones, but different ones covering only the lower half of the side under the chrome accent trim. *Courtesy of the Silva Collection.*

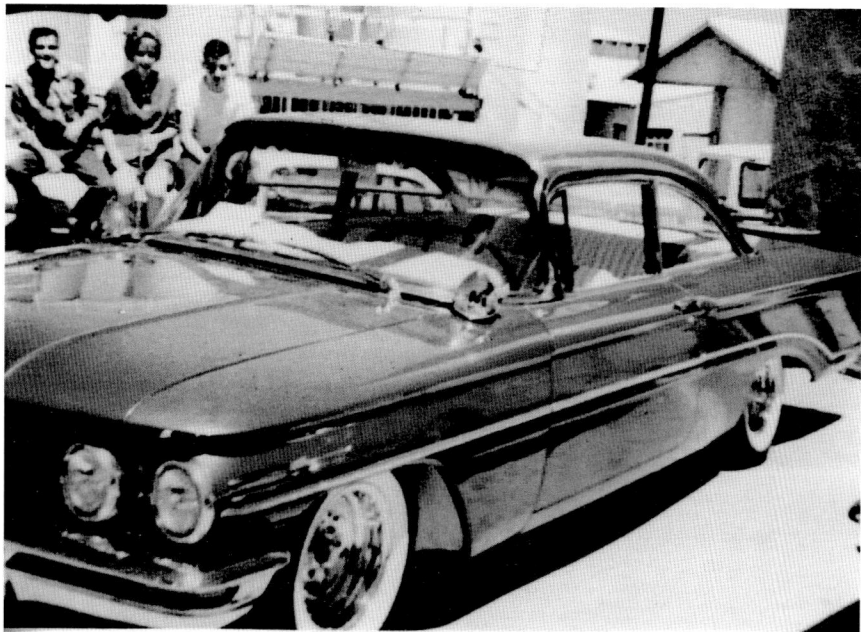

Tipi Del Charo's 1960 Oldsmobile smooth cruiser at the Bauman Motors car show in Rio Vista, California. *Courtesy of the Del Charo Collection.*

The side view of the '52 Chevy accentuates the sloping lines that fade backward from front to rear. The accent paint line follows the roof and truck shape to create lower flow lines. *Courtesy of Tom Cutino.*

The Bill Cabral '58 Oldsmobile is seen on display in Rio Vista at Bauman Motors car show. The beautiful Byer's Metallic Green paint job is highlighted. *Courtesy of the Cabral Collection.*

Wally, Bobby and Donna with Rio Vista in the background. Best friends with really cool custom cars. Nothing better than that. *Courtesy of the Marks Collection.*

Charlie Scholting's '29 Ford Roadster bought from Lenny Byer was his prize possession. *Courtesy of the Byer Collection.*

The 1934 Ford roadster built by Thom Smith at his winery in Herald, California. *Callahan Collection.*

This is the finished roadster pickup by Lenny Byer and Dave Dias. *Courtesy of Dave Dias.*

Car show at the Bass Derby in Rio Vista. Wildfire is displayed with everything open. This is customizing at its finest. *Callahan Collection.*

After all the changes and modifications, this track T-style roadster is a tribute to Dennis Lesh's skill and talent of building cars from scratch. *Courtesy of the Lesh Collection.*

BOB DRON

1950 CHEVROLET HARDTOP

When the name Bob Dron comes up, those who know anything about motorcycles and custom cars are aware of his reputation. He has built over two hundred customs, some of the most amazing, creative vehicles ever made. Bob came from the small town of Isleton, California, in the middle of the Sacramento Delta. He worked for Dron Trucking, the family business. This '50 Chevy was his very first car. Since his family was in the trucking business, he got a hardship driver's license at fifteen and a half. These were issued so that a young man, suitably trained, could operate vehicles for the family business.

Your first car is one you don't forget. Bob's 1950 Chevy hardtop was a custom built by the most famous builder in the Delta: Lenny Byer. The parts for the conversion came from unusual places; the grille surround was from a '53 Chevy, with a grille bar from a '55 Olds bumper guard. They were molded in and the hood fit to it with rounded corners. The bumper was frenched by removing the mounting bolts, filling the holes and welding them to the back so the bumper would be completely smooth. The '50 Ford headlight frame with '53 Ford lenses was also frenched in. Moving back, a crease was added, and the corners were rounded, with the back bumper smoothed and frenched. The taillights were from a '50 Ford molded in low. Lenny sanded and prepped the car for a beautiful lacquer "Honduras Maroon" paint job. The engine originally was a 216-cubic-inch six-cylinder with a split manifold. Mac's Upholstery in Isleton covered the interior in red and white Naugahyde.

Bob Dron's 1950 Chevy was his first car, bought when he was fifteen and a half. He had Lenny Byer do the all the customizing. *Courtesy of Bob Dron.*

It was a flashy car with wide whitewall tires and original '56 Olds three bar spinner hubcaps.

After all this time, Bob is still working on cars and motorcycles. He confirmed, "I haven't quit working on cars." His designs and styles and craftsmanship are one of a kind.

DON DOZIER

1949 CHEVROLET FOUR-DOOR

I've been writing a lot about cars that were built on ranches and farms in the Delta. Sometimes you took the first car that became available to you for transportation. Four-door sedans weren't a first choice, but you got by with what you had. Don send me a letter about the history of his 1949 Chevy. In it, he tells about living out of town and being a hot-rodder:

ON THE CAR, BY DON DOZIER

On the car, it was a 1949 Chevrolet 4-door. I wanted a 2-door Ford with a flathead V-8 but my dad overruled. We bought the car, I think from Jack Bauman Ford in Rio Vista (a trade-in). I needed a car because we had no bus pickup out our way and I started to play football in my sophomore year. My dad said that if I made the team, I would have to get a car as my mom couldn't make another trip to town to pick me up. I decided I would either make the football team (junior varsity) or would definitely die trying!!! I was able to get a driver's license before 16 because we lived in the country. I could just drive my sister and I to school, do grocery shopping for mom and come home. No main street dragging yet for me until I turned 16. I guess I was the only 14-year-old with his own car although I couldn't do anything with it.

Don Dozier's '50 Chevy outside, in front of the barnyard. Another country boy from the ranch who made it into a hot rod. *Courtesy of Don Dozier.*

I had the car through high school until I left to join the Marine Corps in July of 1958. I did all the body work on the car and it was a work-in-progress until the end. The hood was molded, fender strips removed and filled in, lots of other little odds and ends. One of the fellows that worked on the ranch during the summer had been a body and fender man in another life and taught me all about gas welding, working lead, etc. Lots of trials and errors on that old car but it looked pretty good. It was all primer paint when the picture was taken and that was the way it was sold after I left. I did not ever have the money for a paint job. Interior was just good seat covers from Pep Boy's. The engine was stock with the exception of a dual exhaust system with 12" Rocket-tone mufflers that would rattle the windows anytime, anywhere. I didn't have any money for any "speed" gear as such. I bought a dual-carb manifold at one point but could never get the linkage synced up, so I went back to a single stock carb. I was always tinkering with things on the engine and I fabricated a very short capped straight pipe out of both exhaust pipes. I found out that with the pipes uncapped (straight exhaust) and the ignition set way back on the retarded side, the engine would thump, bang and rock like something really bad. We used to go to the drags at Kingdon, park in the area where you pared up with another racer, pull the pipes, set the ignition back and sit on the hood with that six thumping, banging and rocking the car back and forth. The high point of that exercise was me bluffing out a guy with a '50 Mercury/Old's V-8. He stopped by and asked what I had. "Just stock", I said, want to have a go??? His comment was that no way that was stock and he declined to race. He kept asking what I had so I popped the hood and there sat this little stock 6-cylinder Chevy, 1 carb and a lot of "noise"!!! We all had a good laugh about that one.

I was in the Levee Lopers pretty much all the time I was in school. As I said before, I left 2nd gear at Kingdon strip on the last time I raced there. My dad sold the car for me after I left home in 1958 and I have no idea where it went. He probably sold it back to Bauman Motors.

RANDY FERNANDEZ

1956 CHEVROLET TWO-DOOR POST

Pictures of cars seem to look the best when taken low to the ground. Randy's '56 certainly has the look rodders try to achieve. The two-tone paint job follows the chrome trim midway along the body line. George Amaral painted the car Black Berry and Gold Pearl.

Randy Fernandez was a fan of flames, not the big ones, but different ones covering only the lower half of the side under the chrome accent trim. *Courtesy of the Silva Collection.*

JOEY AND FRANK FERREIRA

1923 FORD ROADSTER,
AMERICA'S MOST BEAUTIFUL ROADSTER

The Ferreira brothers, Joey and Frank, bought the roadster from Augie Correia in Rio Vista and drove it around locally. The lived about a block from me, and I saw it all the time as they drove past my Main Street home.

The Ferreira brothers Frank and Joey show their roadster, a different version of the original car, at the Bauman Motors car show. Fenders were added and big, fat, whitewall tires. *Courtesy of Joey Ferreira.*

They entered it in local car shows and the Lodi Customcade show in 1960. Even though it was a nationally known roadster, it was still driven there. While they owned the car, it appeared on the cover of *Car Craft* magazine in June 1980. It was common to see it around; a friend told me she learned to drive a stick shift in that car, cruising around the neighborhood. We didn't realize the important history of it. It was a sporty red car that was fun to race around the Montezuma Hills roads that led to Birds Landing, past the roads leading to gas wells. In the June 1960 *Car Craft* feature, there were three pictures of the roadster with its motorcycle fenders, wide whitewall tires and spinner hubcaps.

NINI FEVEREIRO

1950 CHEVROLET COUPE/1955 CHEVROLET HARDTOP

Nini (Anibal) is a car guy with vast knowledge about local cars and the guys who built them. He has helped me with facts and information for the 2003 calendar and this book. His brother Arthur built the pictured 1950 Chevrolet Sports Deluxe Coupe. It was painted a Ford color: Dust Rose with a white top. All unnecessary emblems and chrome were eliminated and smoothed out. There were twin Appleton spotlights and custom fender skirts with big whitewall tires and '53 Oldsmobile hubcaps. It ran a 235-cubic-inch six-cylinder engine with dual carburetors. The rear of the car was lowered, a popular look in those days. The next car he customized was a 1955 Chevrolet.

Arthur Fevereiro, Nini's older brother, with his first custom car, which he drove to high school. *Courtesy of Nini Fevereiro.*

Top: This side shot of Nini Fevereiro's '55 is just right. It's just lowered just enough, not to low or too high. Profiles are one of the most important factors of a custom car, and he got it right. *Courtesy of Nini Fevereiro.*

Bottom: The smooth lines from front to back end in peaked Packard taillights. This is what you look for in a cool custom. Nini Fevereiro proudly displays his Levee Loper plaque on the rear package shelf. *Courtesy of Nini Fevereiro.*

Nini wanted to re-create the '55 Chevy his brother had Lenny Byer's shop build for him while he was in high school. Unfortunately, Arthur was involved in a fatal accident, and the car was destroyed. Nini wanted to re-create the original car in every detail and began looking for a clone car. He found a car that was the right year and body—a very cherry black '55 Chevy—and bought it from a kid who was driving down the road. Nini actually followed the guy home to Placerville and convinced the owner to sell it to him for

$10,000, which in '83 was a serious piece of change. He contacted Lenny Byer and asked him to re-create his work on Art's car. Lenny accepted the challenge, and made every effort to clone the car, calling on his remarkable skill with lead and torch.

Out front, the headlights were frenched with a nice peak down the center of the hood. Appleton spotlights on either side of the windshield sit in down position. The grille surround was molded in with a Corvette thirteen-teeth grille. Nini hopped up the engine with a 327-block ported and polished heads with a Comp Cam 10:1, TRW's and '57 Vette dual quads built for him by Rick Squalia, whose dad, Rico, built the original. It has a Muncie four-speed and twelve-bolt rear end. It's dropped with two-inch Williams classic spindles and '76 Chevelle discs and rotors. The Packard taillights with a '56 Chevy back bumper and shaved trunk finished the back.

Lenny was called on again to shoot the '51 Buick Maroon paint. Mac's Upholstery stitched the original car's interior and trunk. Nini found former employees to replicate the tuck and roll. Not to be missed are the wide whitewall tires with '57 Dodge Lancer spinner hubcaps. The license plate

The Nini Fevereiro Autorama display with an important view point in the judging process. A car must be opened up for maximum points. The hood, doors and trunk are open for close inspection. *Courtesy of Nini Fevereiro.*

From the balcony at the Sacramento Autorama, the view captures the beautiful display and surrounding area. *Courtesy of Nini Fevereiro.*

is a vintage yellow plate—ARTZZ55—it says it all. Nini has won awards in numerous car shows around the state, including:

Grand National Roadster Show 1990: First in Class and outstanding custom and KKOA Koolest Kemp trophy
Sacramento Autorama
Goodguys Car Show
Woodland Car Show

One of Nini's favorite shows is the Rio Vista Bass Derby car show in October, and he tries to make it when he can.

BOB FRITTS

1958 CHEVROLET IMPALA

Bob lived on a ranch in Birds Landing, a small town with a post office (founded in the 1800s) and a store. He was another boy from a ranch who got an early driver's license at fifteen and a half. His dad got him a '58 Chevy on sale at Travis Air Force Base. Bob did what others did when they started customizing the car: he went to Lenny Byer. He said he listened to Lenny's advice on what do and envisioned exactly what it would look like. First was removing unnecessary chrome lettering but leaving the V front and back because it looked cool. The color would be Candy Apple Green with white accent lines around all edges, all fogged

Bob Fritts's 1958 Chevy at Bauman Motors car show. The '58 Chevy had a huge grille that looked better with the tube grille than stock. Wide and low was the result of the lowering job. *Courtesy of Bob Fritts.*

in. The grille was changed to five tubular bars that fit the front profile perfectly, wide and low. Low because the coils were cut—the car was lowered to ticket level, of which he got several. The interior was stitched in green and white tuck and roll, completed at a shop in Antioch. Then the finishing touches were full-length lake pipes and wide whitewall tires with chrome rims. Next came the very cool Appleton spotlights. The big block 348-cubic-inch V-8 was hopped up for the occasional drag race. Another '58 Impala became famous in the movie *American Graffiti*, but I guarantee you Bob Fritt's '58 was cooler.

ARNOLD GOUVEIA

1955 FORD CONVERTIBLE, 1923 FORD ROADSTER

Arnold is pictured here in his 1955 Ford convertible at the high school. He did all the body work, and George Amaral painted the car Peacock Pink. This was Arnold's transportation throughout high school.

This roadster is truly a backyard build. It started in Arnold's backyard garage with a frame from a Model A Ford. The body was a fiberglass shell. He gathered parts from all around the area. In Lodi, he found the radiator and grille shell. He got parts from Charlie's C&S Auto Parts, including the 283 Chevy engine that he hopped up with a Corvette Cam and pistons. The chromed front axle was from a Ford Model A and Volkswagen tires all around with chrome rims and inch-wide whitewalls and baby moon

Arnold Gouveia's '55 Ford convertible was his high school ride. Painted pink and white and lowered, of course. Add the long drag pipes and 557 Appleton spotlights, and you have a long, low ride. *Courtesy of Arnold Gouveia.*

Arnold Gouveia's '23 Roadster is proof that quality craftsmanship brings rewards. Trophies are the hardware of what other people think of your work. Enough said! *Courtesy of Arnold Gouveia.*

hubcaps. All steering linkage received the chrome treatment along with a modified beer keg for the gas tank. He won awards at the Sacramento Autorama, San Jose and Lodi car shows. He kept it for three or four years and sold it in Galt. It could still be driving around somewhere today; I wouldn't be surprised.

GEORGE LIRA

1923 FORD ROADSTER PICKUP

George's roadsters are a classic example of a design that was a very popular in the 1960s. They remain that way today. Roadster pickups were sometimes similar in appearance, but it pretty much ends there. There are many still around that show up at local and big-name car shows. They are difficult to drive because the rear tires are usually gigantic, with few grooves.

George Lira's roadster is pictured parked on the lawn of the family home. *Courtesy of George Lira.*

This front end is another fine roadster of George Lira's. He is very fond of them, and these two are definitely for someone who can handle them. *Courtesy of George Lira.*

The forward tires are usually a thin motorcycle-type tire specially designed for roadsters with wire wheels. You sit upright with a straight floor-mounted steering column. The roadster usually is about two thousand pounds (one ton), which is very light for the enormous engine. George is a fan of these kinds of cars.

LYLE JESSEE

1950 OLDSMOBILE ROCKET 88

One of the earliest hot rods in Rio Vista, the '50 Oldsmobile was a very sleek car for its time. It had an advanced overhead-valve high-compression V-8 engine and was considered the first muscle car. Lyle Jessee bought one in 1953 and did a very unusual modification for its time. A stock exhaust tail pipe usually exits underneath the car and extends below the rear bumper. Lyle chose to relocate the tailpipe to exit through the taillights. The reflector below the lens was drilled out for the exhaust

The Lyle Jessee 1948 Oldsmobile is one of the best examples of what early customizing was really like. A near stock-looking car with a souped-up motor and fancy paint job. *Courtesy of Lyle Jessee.*

Back side of Lyle Jessee's Oldsmobile with a custom exhaust refitted to exit through the tail light. Cool, huh? *Courtesy of Lyle Jessee.*

pipe. He painted the car a 1953 Oldsmobile Baltic Blue (M). Lyle had the car while in the Marine Corps in San Diego when it was rear ended in a collision. Sadly, that was the end of the road for the car, but with pictures, it lives on. Lyle was an original member of the Gear Jammers Car Club, the first in Rio Vista.

NORMAN "WALLY" MARKS

1955 CHEVROLET

Norman "Wally" Marks bought his very first car while he was still in high school. He was seventeen years old and wanted his own custom car. It remained stock for a very short time before he started customizing it. As mentioned before, customizing required a visit to Bauman Motors Ford dealership to talk to Lenny Byer. The first thing was the removal of chrome ornaments on the hood and trunk and using lead to smooth it out. The primer spots on the car announced the changes being made as sure as a sign. The stock grille was removed, and a Corvette grille was added and

Wally Marks poses with his '55 Chevy. The style changes are not easily noticed because they blend in. Sometimes, simplicity brings out the best in a car. *Courtesy of Norman Marks.*

fit perfectly in the space. It was lowered all around to set the stance, and Lenny prepped and painted the car a '53 Corvette Lime Green. Wally took it went to Isleton for upholstery at Mac's, and full-length drag pipes were added along with spinner hub caps. Wally drove the car while attending Sacramento City College and Sacramento State University. After that, he sold the car to a friend in Rio Vista.

WALT ROSELINI

1950 FORD

Walt is pictured with his 1950 Ford. He is dressed in the clothes popular in those days: a T-shirt with rolled up sleeves and Levi pants. The license plate appears to be from about 1951, yellow on black. This is the only picture found of his early hot rod Ford—hope it brings back some memories.

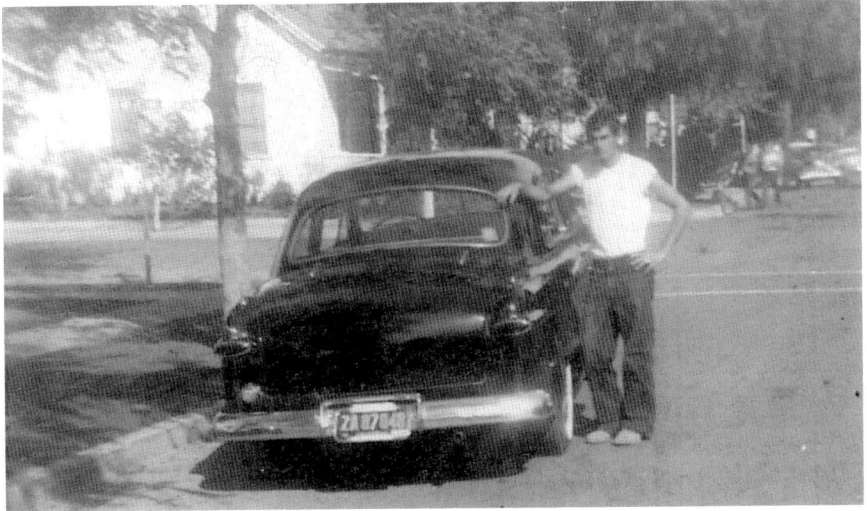

Walt Roselini poses with his 1950 Ford hardtop in a white T-shirt and Levi's jeans, the uniform of the day. *Courtesy of the Rosellini Collection.*

ERNIE LUCAS

1963 DODGE/1939 CHEVROLET COUPE

Ernie Lucas moved to Rio Vista in 1959. The family came from San Rafael when his dad received a job at Blackwelder's Manufacturing. Ernie attended Rio Vista High School and was interested in building hot rods and racing. In those days, a teenager could buy a car for a reasonable amount of money, get his friends together and start building a hot rod. Ernie bought a 1939 Chevy coupe from Jack Dillon in 1960 while still in high school and set to work to turn it into a race car. It had a "really nice" Metallic Blue paint job, and the body and interior were in pretty good shape. He raced it regularly at nearby Kingdon Drag Strip and other nearby tracks. He settled in Oregon and operated a farm.

His appetite for racing continued with a 1963 Dodge Polara "Max Wedge" Super Stock clone car. It could achieve 125 miles per hour. Besides farming, Ernie did car repairs in his garage when he was not traveling around to drag strips in Idaho, Washington and Oregon. He continued working on hot rods and customs until he passed away in 2015.

This image of three guys working under a 1939 Chevy coupe is similar to other pictures of guys working on hot rods that have appeared in the world of hot rod magazines. It was a time when novice car builders got together to simply make a car go faster. Ernie wrote me a letter in 2002 in which he described working on the Chevy:

> *Left to right, me under the front fender, and Zeb Fitch and Dale Sunderman next to me. The car was just bought from Jack Dillon, and we were checking*

Ernie Lucas shows his teenage dreams of racing became a reality with his Polara on a drag strip. *Courtesy of Ernie Lucas.*

This is an iconic picture of its time: three teenagers working together on a summer day making a hot rod. *Courtesy of Ernie Lucas.*

out the best way to remove the 6-cylinder engine and drive train. The car was then equipped with a Pontiac V8 out of a wrecked '58 Bonneville with a Cadillac LaSalle 3-speed manual transmission, and an Oldsmobile rear end. I did almost all the work myself, with the help of Zed, Dale and Victor Mershon. The coupe was the fastest in the ¼ mile in the area for almost a year and a half, until I got in trouble street racing in San Luis Obispo at Cal Poly, my first year in college. My folks made me sell the car after that. I sure had fun while it lasted though. P.S. The picture of the coupe also has Zeb's Model A Ford Roadster and Dale's motorcycle in the background.

JIM MORRIS

1951 CHEVROLET HARDTOP

Jim bought his '51 Chevy from Jack Molino Chevrolet in Walnut Grove. He paid $500 for it and intended to build a custom car. The postmaster there had bought a new '58 Chevy Impala and traded in the '51. Jim took it to the family ranch on Ryer Island. He had his friend Manny Fernandez do some of the bodywork and sprayed a nice light green paint job. He then did what almost every one of his friends did and went to Mac's of Isleton for the upholstery work. Jim had the car until he went away to school at the University of Arizona. He lived in Lodi at the time and gave the car to his cousin Marvin, who got rid of the car, and it disappeared. When Jim returned to the area, he searched everywhere for the car with no luck. So, what do you do when that happens? You have a couple of choices: build a model car of it or build a clone. He started looking for another '51 Chevy to re-create the original.

The project started when Jim got a call from a friend in Las Vegas telling him a nice '51 Chevy hardtop was on display at Silver State Motors. Needless to say, he went over, forked out $6,000 and bought it right there. The custom process began with lowering the car. This was done by de-arching the rear springs and lowering the front spindles. The hood is two pieces, so it was welded together, leaded and primered. The door handles were removed, and electric buttons were installed under the door on the frame, again primered. Moving forward to the front end, the headlights were frenched. The next custom feature was the addition of original '56 Packard taillights, which Jim found at a Pomona swap meet. This is a

Left: Taillights on Jim's '51 are Packard are one of the most popular features used on a custom car. The retro flair and style is still super cool. *Courtesy of Jim Morris.*

Below: The Jim Morris interior is about as classic as you can get, all white. From the headliner to the floor mats, its rich-looking Naugahyde is elegance at its very best. *Courtesy of Jim Morris.*

Jim Morris's 1951 Chevy gets it right with lots of chrome and a pretty Candy Green. *Courtesy of Jim Morris.*

difficult job because lining them up is critical. Jim turned to Gabe's body shop to complete the task. Gabe was a fabricator for George Barris in LA. The interior was next in line, and if you are a fan of white interiors, this is it, white tuck and roll.

Although Jim is a So Cal man now, he frequently returns to Rio Vista to attend to the family ranch. The stock 216-CC engine was replaced with a 302 GMC with a four-barrel carburetor, and Fenton headers completed the engine. He painted it Candy Green, and the restoration of a memory became a reality.

TWIG SILVA

1923 FORD PANEL

Twig's panel roadster is aptly named Rapid Transit. Roadsters are notorious for having gigantic engines pushing a lightweight vehicle. No exception here—this baby is powered by a Chevy 350-cubic-inch engine that was bored and ported with dual Holly carburetors, tunnel rammed and an Isky cam. It used a Mallory ignition and Sanderson exhaust pipes.

Twig Silva's panel really catches your eye with its bright yellow paint, shiny brass fittings and gold leaf lettering. It would be hard to miss this one on the drag. *Courtesy of the Silva Collection.*

The front end was a Dan Woods coil front suspension with motorcycle wheels and tires. The transmission is an automatic three-speed turbo TH400. In the back is a chromed '66 Jaguar rear end. It mounted huge, grooved, street-legal tires and mag wheels. The body is a '23 Ford that was transformed into a delivery-style truck by local body and paint man George Amaral. He constructed the back of the body and added oval side opera-style windows and finished it with a striking Chrome Yellow paint job and antique-looking round brass headlights and matching taillights. The brass theme was carried further with an enormous brass radiator and shroud with flying gull wing smooth moto-meter around a thermometer.

Frank Mills was called on the do the gold leaf lettering and pin-striping. The roadster was taken to Action Interiors for a stitched black diamond-style interior. It was finished with a handmade oak dashboard with Stewart Warner gauges.

CHARLIE SCHOLTING

C&S AUTO PARTS

Just about everyone in the Delta went to Charlie's place, C&S Auto Parts, on River Road going toward Ryer Island. He was in business for himself when he was in high school, and building cars requires a place to go to find parts. He had wrecker trucks for picking up traffic collisions and exchanging vehicles between others doing the same thing. His business card said: Container Rental & Sales, Fork Lift Rentals and Pipe, and car parts.

He bought a1929 Ford Model A roadster from Lenny Byer and took a lot of pride owning that car. It was a show winner at the Oakland Roadster Show and Sacramento Autorama.

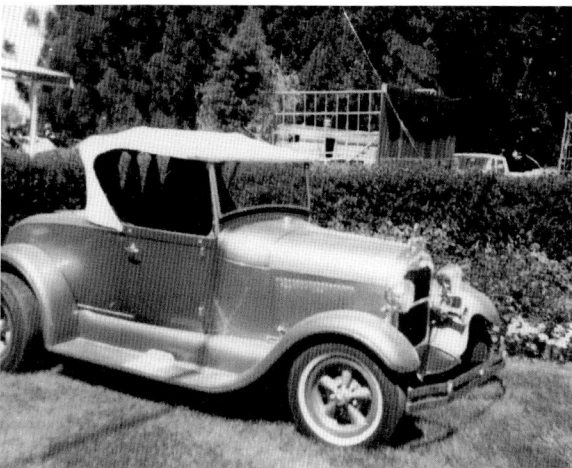

Charlie Scholting's '29 Ford Roadster bought from Lenny Byer was his prize possession. *Courtesy of the Byer Collection.*

DOUG SCHAFER

1954 CHEVROLET PICKUP

You don't see that many pickups customized like Doug's '54 Chevy Truck. It is a well-planned design that works with the unusual body lines of a truck. It didn't start out to be a custom; it was to be a delivery vehicle for Schafer's Department Store. His dad, Art, paid $500 and kept the title, which turned out to be a bad idea. Two of Isleton's body shop men from H.R. Dunn and Son's, Dale "Slim" Kamen and Ron "Boots" Heath, were responsible for the body work.

The first thing I noticed when looking at this extremely clean-looking truck was the headlights. I can't remember ever seeing '57 Chevy headlights

Doug Schafer's Chevy pickup has '57 Chevy headlight buckets, a great look for the front end. *Courtesy of the Schafer Collection.*

Above: Doug Schafer's pickup front: the open hood displays a clean engine compartment painted white for better visibility. *Courtesy of Schafer Collection.*

Left: Doug Schafer's red-and-white interior was done by Mac's Upholstery in Isleton. *Courtesy of the Schafer Collection.*

used as he did. It is a big one-piece unit with a single light surrounded by a bezel that projects into a chisel shape to enhance the dynamic look.

The grille area is stock yet cleaned and filled and re-chromed to brilliance. The back end of the truck bed has a completely molded-in bumper with new taillights reformed in oblong shape housing dual bullet-shaped lenses. The engine compartment is neat and painted a clean white. The chrome is tastefully done, with functionality in mind. Doug wanted to show the truck but race it as well. The interior is awesome; tuck and roll white is the theme with red accents.

The dashboard is also cool tuck and roll. The Chevy has a chrome dashboard and long, straight shifter. Attention to detail is apparent when you look at just one of the seemingly small things he did: the inside windshield is chromed, as is the single seat support. The intention to race is evident by the important seat belts and racing slicks in the rear. All tires are whitewalls, and sometimes practicality works best when racing: simple black rims with chromed nuts give it a drag racing presence. Doug's truck was raced at Kingdon Drag strip in Lodi. He had an award for the fastest truck in its class. He attended Delta College and University of the Pacific and was drafted into the armed forces. He served in the U.S. Navy as a yeoman submariner. Doug's father, Art, sold the truck while he was away with the navy. They had spent over $4,000 fixing up his truck. For Christmas in 1960, Doug's present from his dad was a toy red truck with a tag that read:

1 Pickup Red: $500.00
Parts & Labor & Headaches: $3,729.33
Total: $4,229.33
Too Much
12/25/60

JACK SCHAFER

1932 FORD FIVE-WINDOW COUPE

The '32 Ford coupe is perhaps one of the most iconic cars in the hot rod era. It was immortalized by a song and a movie. The song "Little Deuce Coupe" was a terrific hit for the Beach Boys. Then along came the movie *American Graffiti*. Its main car star was John Milner's yellow chopped deuce coupe. Jack's "Little Deuce Coupe" was way before the movie came out but iconic in its own right. He was a lucky young man; the coupes were called the backbone of the postwar hot-rodding movement because of the beautiful lines and light weight. Jack's dad, Ebner "Shorty" Schafer, brought him the car bought from his aunt and uncle in Lodi. It was a 1932 Ford Coupe Model B with a four-cylinder, fifty horsepower from 201 cubic inches. During the time he worked on the deuce, two different engines powered it. The original factory stock motor was pulled and replaced with a 1953 Mercury flathead engine.

There are several things that need to happen to make the stock '32 into a true hot rod, and the first is a top chop. This was done in a Sacramento body shop by Jack F. Silva. He was also responsible for the body work. Next is lowering the profile, and a three-inch dropped axle took care of the proper stance. It ran on whitewall tires and '56 Old's Fiesta Spinner hubcaps. His dad and uncle took the car to a body shop in Lodi to get it painted and upholstered. The paint chosen was 1955 Ford Victoria Regency Purple. It was moved over to the upholstery part of the shop for a custom job. The result was a blue and white Naugahyde seat and door panels. The roof was pleated white Naugahyde. The dash got new gauges

Jack Schafer's '32 Deuce under construction. The chopped top gives it a solid look. *Courtesy of the Schafer Collection.*

The nose of Jack's Deuce shows the nice reflection of the Regency Purple paint. *Courtesy of the Schafer Collection.*

Left: The full front of the '32 gives a great look at the profile coming directly at you. *Courtesy of the Schafer Collection.*

Below: The engine compartment with the hood and side panels off show a large space for the engine. *Courtesy of the Schafer Collection.*

and a white steering wheel. The finishing touch was upholstered white running boards.

The engine was replaced by a Dodge 241 Red Ram Hemi with 140 horsepower and a two-barrel carburetor. Jack drove his '32 as a daily driver going to college and was a member of the Levee Lopers car club. In 1959, Jack entered the Lodi Road Angels Car Club Customcade Car Show in Lodi. There were two other entries from the Levee Lopers: #252 Bill Cabral, 1958 Oldsmobile, and #701 Frank Anadoe Ferreira, 1927 Model-T roadster. Jack won second place in his category.

THOM SMITH

1954 CHEVROLET, 1934 FORD ROADSTER

Thom was a friend and a really cool guy with a '54 Chevy. I remember the first time I saw it in 1965 in Rio Vista. I had just got out of the army, and he was driving the '54 all over the place. It was a mild custom lowered with baby moons and chrome reversed rims. He said the color was Mack Truck Orange. I had a '50 Chevy coupe that I painted '65 Mustang Orange, so when we went to cruise the drags together our cars stood out. Thom and a friend are pictured here at the University of the Pacific in Stockton doing what they usually did: talk to college girls.

The 1934 Ford Roadster built by Thom Smith at his winery in Herald, California. *Callahan Collection.*

Thom Smith and friend at the University of the Pacific in Stockton. *Courtesy of the Smith Collection.*

Thom started working on the '34 in the late '60s. Charlie Scholting, who owned the local wrecking yard, had most of the basic supplies, including the frame, axles front and back and transmission. The engine was from a '69 GMC truck and had throttle-body fuel injection. Thom also put in a sweet set of headers that gave it the proper sound of a hot rod.

Thom was the kind of guy who didn't go along with current trends. Where everyone built or wanted to build a '32 deuce coupe or roadster, he built a '34. He bought, arguably, the best fiberglass body and fenders in the market and put together a very nice roadster. We talked about me buying the car, even settled on a price, when he passed away as a result of an accident on his ranch. I eventually brought the roadster and finished the car. He wanted to show it at the Sacramento Autorama, and I did: second place in class.

AL AND JANE THURMAN

1931 FORD SEDAN

This '31 can be classified as a survivor. It was originally built by Rico Squalia in Walnut Grove. It was a show car that made it to the Oakland National Roadster show.

A young Ron "Boots" Heath is pictured with the '31 Ford. Rico's name is featured on the placard for entry number 355, street sedan, at that show. It was chopped and painted purple with a white Naugahyde roof cover, two purple stripes and white running boards.

The car is pictured on a driveway in Lodi. You can see the Naugahyde-upholstered roof and padded running boards. At that time, it still had its original purple paint job, and Rod Rice was the second owner. He acquired the car in 1960 and drove it for two years. Unfortunately, Rod passed away and the car was given to Jane, his sister, in 1965, and she kept it until it was sold in 1971 to Andy Crowe. He hadn't owned it for very long when he blew the transmission racing and subsequently parked it in a barn on Sherman Island, where it sat for four years. The next owner was Arnold Gouveia, who rebuilt it around 1975. He was well known in the Delta as a very good builder and customizer of cars, and the trophies he won over the years prove that point. It remained in Rio Vista for thirty-three years until Arnold talked to Jane. It seems that she made Arnold promise that if he ever sold the car, he would offer it to her first.

Al and Jane Thurman bought it back in February 2006. When asked the price they paid, the response is *plenty*. Of course, you simply can't leave a car alone when it is a street rod. It's usually referred to by the name of the owner

Left: Al and Jane Thurman's 1931 Ford Roadster beginning its transformation to show quality. *Courtesy of the Thurman Collection.*

Below: Thurman's '31 in the home driveway, clean and washed and looking good. *Courtesy of the Thurman Collection.*

Opposite, top: Boots Heath with the '31 originally built by Rico Squalia currently owned by the Thurmans. *Courtesy of the Squalia Collection.*

Opposite, bottom: Rod Rice (Jane's brother) owned the '31 Ford sedan by Rickey Squalia in the '60s when he lived in Lodi. *Courtesy of the Thurman Collection.*

Al Thurman stands proudly by his completed restoration, which means so much to the family. *Courtesy of the Thurman Collection.*

who last built or modified it. The top, for example, was chopped way back in the '60s by Rico Squalia. The chop gives the blocky body style a different lower profile and the look of a hot rod. It was rebuilt with all the modern updates and features to drive the highways at today's speeds. It has a Dark Royal Blue Metallic paint job by Walt's Paint and Body shop by painter Dale McGuinness. The power comes from a 302 Ford with Edelbrock Carbs connected to a C-4 transmission leading to a Jaguar rear end. A Walker radiator keeps the mill cool. There are leaf springs in front with coils in the back, with Wildwood Disc brakes in front and Jaguar Discs in the rear. Wheels are fourteen-inch front and fifteen-inch rear. Inside are Mustang seats in front and an original backseat. They are covered with velour, a plush woven fabric, stitched by Baker's Upholstery in Fairfield.

Al and Jane still own the car and show it regularly at local area car shows. This is a historical car, with an interesting background that goes back over eighty years.

LE AND ROBBY WEBER

1941 FORD SEDAN DELIVERY

A 1941 Ford sedan delivery is a pretty rare vehicle. With America's entry into World War II, all civilian vehicle manufacturing was halted after Pearl Harbor. There were 4,846 delivery sedans delivered in 1941, only the standard model, with a broad feather-styled trim on the front. It is believed that this particular panel was used by the local utilities

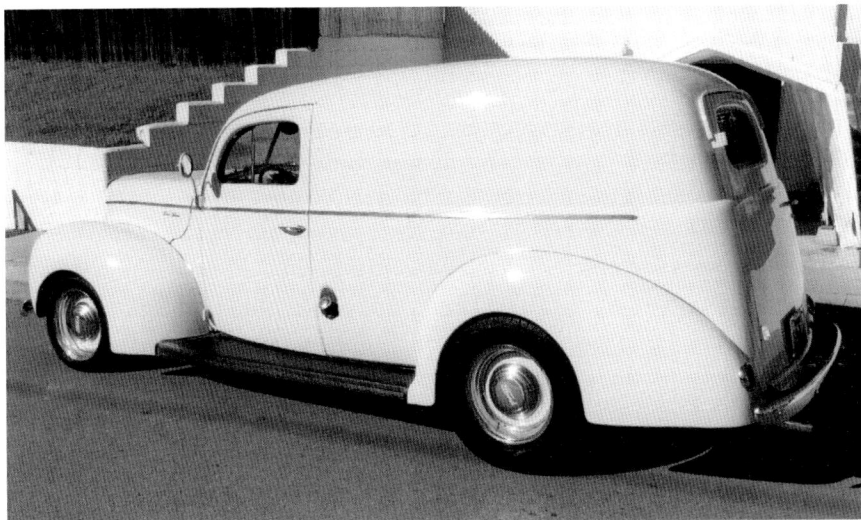

The rear side view of Robbie Weber's '41 Ford is what a very old vehicle can look like when handled with extreme care and given a fine paint job and cool retro wheels. *Callahan Collection.*

Robbie Weber's '41 Ford Sedan Delivery is looking extremely good on a bright sunny day, accentuating the flawless bright-yellow paint job. *Callahan Collection.*

company. It was then sold to the Breland family, which used it for handyman business. Robby's older brother Le Weber bought the panel for $400 and said it was in terrible shape. He had a plan to customize it from the start. Le worked on it in the high school shop, putting on a new hood and all four fenders. His friend Rod Dolk helped him pull the old motor. They went to Sacramento and bought a hopped-up Merc flathead engine and headers for $200, brought it all home and installed them in the panel. Included also in the deal was a dropped axle that would fit, and best of all, it was dropped three inches. Le drove it with a bucket seat—I mean it really was a bucket, until he found a bench seat and tossed the bucket. Lenny Byer also worked on it at Bauman Motors. Dale "Slim" Kamen and Ron "Boots" Heath also did some work. Le went off to college in 1966 and sold the panel to his younger brother Robby. The panel has stayed with the family for the last sixty years. Robby can be seen driving it around town; he has kept it in excellent condition.

DARRYL BATCHELOR

1923 FORD T ROADSTER

This is a classic '60s-style roadster pictured on Front Street at the Rio Vista Bass Derby. The queen is Vicky Bennett and her chariot a 1923 "T" Ford Roadster—built by Darryl Bachelor, who was always into hot rods in high school. He was very good at drawing cars, and most of his class notes included sketches of cars. He took drafting, and after the required stuff was finished, he designed cars. A roadster like his is very difficult to do. It takes a very patient person to design cars as he did because you can't test anything until everything is together. I don't know if Darryl designed the roadster before building it, but looking at it closely, you find many things not done by chance. The chassis is handmade to fit the body, which is about a '23 Ford. It is cut to fit the frame in a position raised a bit in the back, so it sits at a rake. (A rake is having the rear wheels higher than the front, creating a slope to the front.) It is obvious when you look at it, the incline is so pronounced. The windshield is mounted to the body, leaned forward with two support braces bolted to the headlight bracket. Mounted onto the Model T windshield frame are a couple of items to make the car pass the vehicle inspection safety test, including a rearview mirror, round and high up for a clear backward view. A horn is also necessary, so why not follow the theme with a curling brass antique-looking one with a big rubber bulb. Just under the horn are two clearance lights, again antique in style. They look like old lanterns but are the opposite, with electricity and wired for performance. The engine has a big four-barrel carburetor with four exhaust pipes sloping downward and turning back aligned together. Both front and

Darryl Bachelor's '23 Ford roadster has a classic look with lots of brass-plated parts, a chariot for Bass Derby Queen Vicky Bennett. *Callahan Collection.*

rear axles are supported by radius rods for firm alignment. The tie rod and drag link connect to the steering column under the driver's side. Keeping the mill cool is a Brassworks "T" radiator with a Moto-Meter winged radiator cap. The front suspension has a dropped tube axle.

This is a beautiful "T" roadster that was fit for a queen and obviously was a carriage for one. Darryl passed away several years ago. In a questionnaire for our high school reunion, Darryl wrote: "My hobbies are cars and going 135 mph on Highway 12 and also winning the West Coast Hot Rod National 4 years in a row." (No one else ever did that)

He drove his Model T roadster over a quarter of a million miles. RIP, Darryl.

EZRA EHRHARDT

CALIFORNIA HIGHWAY PATROL

Rico Squalia and his son Rick, at the wheel, are seen here at a local car show with their national winning roadster are under the watchful eye of California Highway Patrol (CHP) officer Ezra Ehrhardt. Does it seem odd that a highway patrol officer is included in this book? Well, it isn't when you consider the problems with street and highway racing in California in the '50s and '60s. It seems there was no distinction between hot rods and custom cars in the public eye. Custom cars, as a general rule, were rarely raced, but they did see how fast they could go.

Mild custom car owners were usually inclined to test their vehicles against each other, but not so much those who spent everything on a show car. The CHP commissioner enacted a program to try to stop dangerous racing. The result was appointing two veteran officers to start a new program of education and accountability for the many local car clubs in the state. The state was split into north and south. Ezra Ehrhardt, who lived in Lodi, was appointed to handle the north, and Chuck Pollard the south. They would visit the local drag strips; our local one was Kingdon Airfield in Lodi. On weekends and designated weeknights, it converted into a drag strip. Grudge races, as they were called, were popular, since beefs between two guys could be settled there under supervision and, above all, safety. Kingdon gained much respect because the big names in the sport raced there. Don Garlits with his famous Swamp Rat, T.V. Tommy Ivo, Don "The Snake" Pruhomme and Connie Kaletta all competed there.

Rico and Rick Squalia at a car show, with Officer Erhardt checking out the roadster. *Courtesy of the Squalia Collection.*

The CHP was also going to the biggest car show in the country: the Oakland National Roadster Show. It has been held every year since 1950, although the location has been moved to Pomona, California, in recent times. Originally, it was held in the exhibition building in downtown Oakland. Officer Ezra Ehrhardt, originally a motorcycle patrolman, became a regular fixture at the show in part because of his assignment. The National Hot Rod Association was also working to get street racing onto supervised drag strips and began setting up information booths in the show to recruit and give out safety literature. It was tremendously successful, and when the hall of fame was formed in 1960, Officer Ezra Ehrhardt was inducted as one of the nine charter members. Following in his footsteps, two other officers would be recognized for their service: Lee "Woody" Wood in 1962 and E.J. "Bud" Coons in 1964. Ezra passed away in 1967, and his service to our area was a great part of the roads becoming safe.

PART III

CAR CLUBS AND CAR SHOWS

THE GEAR JAMMERS, RIO VISTA

Lyle Jessee
Buck McPherson
Bill Friedel
Gordy Cordoza
Gary San Filippo
Jim Thomas
Buster Brewer

THE LEVEE LOPERS, RIO VISTA

John Lira Jr.	Manny Lira
Doug Schafer	Arthur Fevereiro
Zeb Fitch	Johnny Correia
Waldo Schmit	Bill Black
Charles Brown	Joe Terry
Jimmy DeFlores	Bill Cabral
Dale Sunderman	Jack Schafer
Norman Brown Jr.	Nini Fevereiro
Bob Simons (advisor)	George Tudhope (advisor)

THE DELTA-CREEPERS, ISLETON

Nini Fevereiro	Johnny Perez
Richard Perez	Bruno Roselini
Terry Emigh	Trinidad Perez
Johnny Borba	Jerry Dron
Johnny Correia	Robert Souris

Plaque images from the Callahan Collection.

THE RIO VISTA BASS DERBY AND CAR SHOW

The Bass Derby first began in 1933 to bring attention to the fishing industry with a contest. Whoever caught the biggest, heaviest striped bass would win the hotly contested event. It was interrupted from 1938 until 1949 because of World War II, but it has continued since then to present day. It is a very big deal in town and has the support of many local clubs and organizations. The Levee Lopers have made numerous appearances over the years, with columns of members parading their custom cars and hot rods.

Pictured here is the staging area on Montezuma Street. Leading the group is a beautiful 1956 Chevy convertible driven by Manny Lira. The car to the left is the '55 Chevy of Arthur Fevereiro. Following him is Johnny Correria's '50 Mercury. Joe Terry's '40 Ford sedan is close behind. Moving to the right of Manny's '56 is John Perez's '53 Ford, then Bill Black's '52 Chevy and Bill Cabral's '54 Ford. Way in the back is the top of Doug Schafer's '54 Chevy truck. This was a goodwill gesture for the local teenagers to show their cars and have the locals see who they were. It wasn't until 1990 that an actual car show was held on Saturday afternoon to attract more interest in the derby. The derby has gained in popularity over the years, changing as it went along

Lining up for a Bass Derby parade, the Levee Lopers car club is well represented. *Callahan Collection.*

to become an even bigger event. Originally called the Rio Rendezvous, the event's name has changed over the past twenty-seven years with different hosts. It's now known as the Bass Derby Car Show and still running strong. I've personally entered my car in the show a number of times, and I can say it is an excellent location down Main Street with a large participation every year. Recently, they have soapbox derby race cars going down Main Street. These are supervised, sanctioned races, of course!

KINGDON DRAG STRIP, LODI, CALIFORNIA

My first visit to see the drags was on March 20, 1960, and it was quite an experience. The big names in the 1960s were Don "Big Daddy" Garlits, Art Malone, Bob Sullivan and T.V. Tommy Ivo. Tommy was in the cast of *The Donna Reed Show* and appeared in many movies and TV shows in the '50s and '60s. He was very popular and a crowd pleaser. He came to the strip that day pulling a trailer carrying two dragsters. Unfortunately, his number one dragster was not running well, so he unloaded the backup, and it was really cool. His cars were usually painted bright red with graphic names and logos, but this one was different. It had a white background with spots all over in a camel pattern. Others said it looked like a lava lamp design, and it ran very well that day. It was a full house, with cars parked everywhere since there was limited pavement available. It was the place to race and regarded as one of the most prominent drag strips on the West Coast.

Kingdon was also part of the National Hot Rod Association certified racing circuit. It is a three-quarter-mile-long stretch of pavement in the middle of farm fields. The first manager of the strip was Robert L. Cress, a Stockton Police officer. It has been said he wrote speeding tickets and told drivers to go to Kingdon, where speeding was encouraged. To win a race there was something and still is. Other CHP officers and local police joined in and also helped. Kingdon also was an active airstrip, and stories abound about the drags being halted and cleared when an airplane needed to land—that must have been a sight, a couple thousand people watching a pilot land. Then it was hurriedly returned to drag racing. Nowadays, Interstate 5 runs nearby, and if you know where it is, it's visible. Back then, there was no I-5, but Highway 12 runs east–west just north of the strip. Kingdon Road, the namesake of the strip, ran on the east side, north to south. Good news is that the drag strip is still in use today; there are a couple of events scheduled a year.

There were a couple of Delta guys who were trophy winners in the '60s. John Lira Jr. was a member of the Levee Lopers, and during his time, he won a couple of trophies there. He drove his black 1958 Chevy two-door post in the class A stock car division. Stories about his feats were included in the *River News Herald*.

John Lira Jr. shows us his original Levee Lopers club jacket. It was with pride they wore these coats. *Courtesy of John Lira Jr.*

John Lira, Jr. Places First in Class A Racing at Kingdon

John Lira, Jr. added another trophy to his collection recently in class A stock car racing at the Kingdon Drag Strip. Lira, who is president of the Levee Lopers, now has five trophies for placing first in class A stock car racing. His elapsed time was 13.86 and top time was 87.86 and top time was 87.5. The youth said that 300 participated in different classes of the race. He stressed that the Levee Lopers are interested in racing on drag strips, not on the highway.

John Lira, Jr. Wins New Laurels in Racing

John Lira, Jr. of Rio Vista, who has speeded to victory in many drag races, gained new laurels last Sunday in Stockton, when he captured to place in his division in the national championships staged by the Central Valley Timing Association. Lira covered a quarter mile in 15.20 seconds for a speed of 91.09 miles per hour to top 34 entries in his class. His victory is regarded in racing circles as an extremely high honor. The president of the Levee Lopers has an array of trophies he has won in drag races. John sent me a letter in which he explains what happened that day at the Kingdon nationals drags.

"I got beat by a 1957 Chevy. I know the guy and he is in the wrong class, he should have been in Super Stock (SS). I was in A Stock, but I needed $100 to protest him so I am going to find $100, I went around and

started collecting $1.00, $5.00 and $10.00 dollars, any amount. I took down names and money. An hour later this guy comes up and asked what happened? Did he beat you, I said yes, but he's in the wrong class. He took the $100 to the officials and that started a brawl, he would not tear down his motor, he was illegal, so I won the trophy and got my $100 back. About a year later at the Antioch drive-in, a guy comes up and asks if my car was for sale. Well I thought, I'm getting tired of racing, so yes but this car is not cheap and has a reputation of being a hell of a lot faster than others like it. He says I know him he lent me money to tear down the '57 Chevy. We met Monday at the bank, done deal!"

I heard from a reliable source of information that every time the Rio Vista Police got a new car, they would meet us at the airport to race. (I guess they wanted to see if it was fast enough to catch a hopped-up hot rod.)

Another notable drag racer from Rio Vista was Arnold Gouveia. A *River News Herald* column noted one of his victories: "A big trophy came home with a Rio Vistan after the Kingdon drag races last Sunday. Proud holder of the honor is Arnold Gouveia, son of Mr. and Mrs. Manuel Gouveia. He captured it for the fastest take-off in the Sunday event."

Don Dozier raced there too. He told me about his last run at Kingdon Drag Strip during the "Tuesday Night Grudge Drags." Don said he raced his car when it was still in gray primer, and he blew up the transmission and left his second gear there. He drove it around until he sold it, without a working second gear.

Bill Cabral also raced at Kingdon Drag Strip in his '54 Ford coupe and won second place in his class.

John Lira Jr.'s brother Manny had a '56 Chevy, and Harry Hansen had a '52 Chevy—they were always challenging each other to a race. Both had hopped-up engines with McCullough superchargers, and they both were very fast. Unfortunately, for whatever reason, they never put the pedal to the metal, but that would have been one hell of a race!

MODEL CAR SHOWS

I remember when we were young kids back in the '50s making model cars. The older boys were getting driver's licenses, buying cars and customizing them. We were too young for that, so we turned to an alternative: customizing plastic cars and trucks. We were able to think creatively and change a regular model car into our own custom car. The early model kits were very crude when compared with the super detailed projects of today. The glue we used came in a tube and took forever (it seemed) to dry. There was liquid bottle and brush glue, but they weren't very good either. Custom kits were few and far between, and when we got one we would trade one another cast parts and chromed pieces. Now they call what we did *kit bashing*. Many of the custom features we wanted to add were not made, so we built them from scratch. Appleton spotlights, a popular feature on real cars, were available, but you would have to buy another kit that had them.

These were the custom ribbons we won at the model car shows. They were very important and appreciated. *Callahan Collection.*

We made our own by using plastic or wood formed into shape, sanded and finished with Testors model silver paint. Lake pipes, or drag pipes as we called them, were made from solder wire, bent to shape and also painted silver. Spray paint was another thing—what was available came from the local variety store. The variety was basic colors in enamel paint.

Model car building accomplished several things that other types of kits didn't. Airplane and train kits were made to be built exactly as the printed instructions. All parts were drawn in simple pictures of how things fit together in a proper progression from start to finish. Each part had a number stamped by it so we could identify them. We learned about following building instructions, but we learned to adapt them to suit our own ideas. At a certain time in the building process, we didn't use instructions at all. In the custom car world, no two cars are exactly alike, yet all production cars have different models—each model is built the same. Customs of the same models are different because it is required. We in model building were able to get kits of certain customs called three-in-one kits featuring stock, semi and full custom. Sameness is the enemy of customizers, and that was the first lesson we learned: to be different, be yourself. I began by making replicas of cars that were driven around town and school. This expanded to using our imagination and skills to build more detailed models.

Actual pictures of our entries in the local model cars show. Judges were local car experts. *Callahan Collection.*

We would all read these articles, and soon model car pictures and stories were regular monthly features. Magazines like *Hot Rod*, *Car Craft* and *Rod & Custom* helped fan the flames of our excitement with the national attention to the art of model cars. It went from playing with toy cars to the serious study of design.

Most of our recreation in Rio Vista and the area took place at the local Youth Center. It was built in 1946, and served as the main meeting place for everything from Boy Scouts to teen dances and sports. The local car club, the Levee Lopers, sponsored a number of the dances and helped put on our model show contests and served as judges.

The *River News Herald* printed the following article about our model car contests:

1958 MINIATURE AUTO SHOW SUCCESSFUL

The "miniature auto show" proved quite a success Al Taylor, a summer recreation director announced last week. Ribbons and prizes were awarded in all categories with two miniature auto kits awarded as prizes to the best full customs cars of the show.

The results of the recreation show.

PICKUP
Full Custom: Bob Weiss 1st, George Amaral 2nd, Ray Terry 3rd
Semi-Custom: Fred Hague 1st, John Callahan 2nd, Frank McGahey 3rd

SEDAN
Full Custom: George Amaral 1st
Semi-Custom: Jim DeFlores 1st, Steve Bigler & Glen McGahey tie 2nd,
Billy Dole & Glen McGahey tie 3rd

STOCK
Mike Lopez 1st, Fred Hague 2nd

COUPE
Full Custom: George Amaral 1st, Ray Terry 2nd, John Callahan 3rd
Semi-Custom: John Callahan 1st, Joe Schmit 2nd

CONVERTIBLES
Full Custom: Bob Weiss 1st, Larry Pelton 2nd
Semi-Custom: Gary Silva 1st, Jim DeFlores 2nd, Fred Sires & Dennis
Ostlund tie 3rd
Stock: Jim DeFlores 1st, Frank McGahey & Mike Lopez tie 2nd, David
Silva & Billy Dole tie 3rd

STATION WAGONS
Full Custom: Fred Sires 1st, Rod Baker 2nd
Semi-Custom: Fred Sires 1st, Skipper Wallace 2nd
Stock: Frank McGahey 1st

The next contest was two years later, and the *River News* also reported on it:

Wednesday, August 19, 1960
George Amaral Sweeps Honors in R.V. Miniature Auto Show
    George Barris Amaral walked off with first, second and third places—
all three—in the best of the show competition in the miniature auto exhibit
staged last week at the youth center under the sponsorship of the City
Recreation Department.

It was pointed out that while it is unusual for one entrant to win all best of show awards, nevertheless, the names were all hidden, and the judges selected the winning cars on a basis of pure workmanship. They complimented young Amaral on his outstanding job. The judges were three local men with knowledge of customizing: Jack Sheehan, "Boots" Heath and John Lira, Jr. There were more class entries in the competition: Pickups, Sedans, Coupes, Convertibles, Station Wagons, Roadsters and Dragsters. 45 models were entered in this contest and following are the complete results.

PICKUP CLASS—Semi Custom: Rick Oglesby 1st, Bob Weiss (Isleton) 2nd, George Amaral 3rd, Steve Adams (special ribbon)
  SEDAN—Stock: Rick Oglesby 1st & 2nd, Jack Dillon, Steve Bigler, (special ribbon)
Semi-Custom: John Callahan 1st, Steve Bigler 2nd, George Amaral 3rd
Full Custom: George Amaral 1st, Jack Dillon 2nd
  COUPE—Stock: Fred Hague 1st, Dennis Ostland 2nd
Semi-Custom: Semi Custom: Ray Miller 1st, Bob Weiss 2nd, Danny Oglesby 3rd
Full Custom: George Amaral 1st, Frank McGahey 2nd,
  CONVERTIBLES—Stock: Rick Oglesby 1st, Steve Bigler 2nd, Larry Davis 3rd
Semi-Custom: Fred Hague 1st, Bob Bird 2nd
Full Custom: Bob Weiss 1st, Steve Bigler 2nd, Bob Hayden 3rd
  STATION WAGONS—Stock: Dennis Mari
Semi-Custom: Steve Bigler 1st, Bob Hayden 2nd
Full Custom: Fred Hague 1st
  ROADSTERS—George Amaral, 1st, 2nd, tie 3rd with Jack Dillon
  DRAGSTERS—John Callahan 1st, Rick Oglesby 2nd, Jack Dillon 3rd
  BEST OF SHOW—George Amaral 1st, 2nd, 3rd

The following article emphasizes the importance in building models. I liked the idea that each of us selected *our* favorite project vehicle. That in itself added to the attractiveness of the event: our ideas, our creativeness, our work.

BUILD MODEL CARS [Hot Rod Magazine, January 2000]
by HRM Staff

There has always been a misconception that model cars are for kids, a silly pastime akin to basket weaving or pottery. Forget that. Short of actually working on real cars, there is no better way to learn about automotive engineering than to assemble as many car model kits as you can. Painted and detailed or just tossed together straight from the box, the construction process is much like that of a real car. And as you begin modifying and customizing, you'll be exposed to the basic engine swapping, axle narrowing, the critical impact of the wheel and tire selection, not to mention body and paint work. For me, the old IMC Little Red Wagon Kit (recently re-released by Lindberg) is a revelation. With opening doors and detailed recreation of the ingenious engine and suspension cradle used on the real truck, this kit is a shining example of how indispensable educational tool, regardless of how old that calendar on the wall says you are.

RIO VISTA HIGH SCHOOL AUTO SHOP CLUB

The auto shop class of 1960 had a project roadster pickup. It was ongoing, and it seems most everyone worked on it in one way or another. The instructor was Calvin Krienke. He was a big man, towering over just about every student in his classes. He did not intimidate anyone; just the opposite, everyone liked him, and affectionately called him "Mr. Krink." (He was an army veteran of World War II who flew a B-24s on combat missions.) He started a class project car and instead of teaching about an old stripped-down junk car no one was interested in, he did something different. Mr. Krink started them working on a hot rod pickup. The car was always in primer paint, and many of the parts were brought to school by the students. The Model A body and frame were donated from unknown sources, but the original Cadillac motor was donated by Gilbert Moreno. It was later replaced by an Oldsmobile motor. All the guys drove it one time or another, and it was licensed. Bobby Hadden told me he used drive it to the A&W root beer stand during class hours. They were never stopped, and the root beer run became a frequent method of road testing. When Mr. Krink moved to Lodi, he took it with him; it was seen driving around town there but disappeared forever. Pictured here are pupils registered in the class, and when the rumor went around about the school picture's day, several opportunists showed up to be in the photos. At least that's what someone told me.

The high school auto shop group outside the shop entrance. *Courtesy of Rio Vista High School.*

GET TOGETHER PICTURES

AROUND THE DELTA

One of the things the guys and gals like to do was get together, usually on the weekend, to take pictures. Since picture taking was done with an old-time camera with actual film that was loaded by hand, few were taken. After taking the shots, you had to take the film to the drugstore and wait a week for them to be developed and returned. It was expensive, and you had to pay for the ones that didn't turn out.

THREE FRIENDS GOT TOGETHER one weekend long ago to wash and polish their cars at Beaver Union School in Walnut Grove and took a group picture of their custom cars. Three different years of Chevrolet in each guy's different choice, but equal beauty. To the left is the wide and low-to-the-ground '60 Chevy of Rich Gemignani. It had Candy Apple Red paint by Bertolucci's Body Shop in Sacramento. The car came with a nice red-and-white stock interior. He had Rico Squalia drop it down and was ever watchful that Deputy Simoni didn't ticket him. The stock grille was replaced with a tube bar grille. The wheels had whitewall tires with the coolest hubcaps ever made: 1956 Oldsmobile Fiesta Spinners. In the center is Rick Squalia's White 1957 Chevy. It had all emblems removed and molded in and lowered to a rake. The engine was a 265-cubic-inch V-8 with a cam and twin four-barrel carburetors. To the right is Nini Fevereiro's smooth '55 Chevy. It's painted a '51 Buick Maroon with wide whitewall tires and Olds Fiesta Spinner hubcaps. It was a beautiful day in the Delta and made for a great picture.

Rich Gemignani's '60 Chevy, Rick Squalia's '57 Chevy and Nini Fevereiro's '55 Chevy. *Courtesy of the Marks Collection.*

SCENIC LOCATIONS COULD BE found at the river or the high school. Parks were popular too. Black and white was normal, but color was better and cost more, so they did what they could. Those with parents who had photography as a hobby usually had the best quality pictures. This location is at Rio Vista High

School looking downward toward town. The two cars belong to Norman "Wally" Marks, the '55 Chevy on the right, and Walt "Waldo" Schmit, '57 Ford on the left. Wally stands between the two cars where Donna Jeffrey (*left*) and Bob Nunes (*right*) are holding hands. Maybe Walt is the one taking the picture?

Schmit's '57 Ford and Marks's '55 Chevy. *Courtesy of the Marks Collection.*

TWO BEAUTIFUL ROADSTERS BY the Sacramento River. On the left is the Jack Coughlin '32 Ford roadster. Notice its stance, aggressive, like it's ready to jump over the starting line—basic black waiting for the flag. Next to it is Lucky Silva's '32 roadster pickup with a much lower stance, powerful. The angle of the picture frames the cars slightly below the camera.

Jack Coughlin's '32 Ford Roadster and Lucky Silva's '32 Ford Pickup. *Courtesy of Danny Kamen.*

PICTURE THE YEAR: 1987, and three guys from Rio Vista drive up to a Murphy, California car show. It's about an hour and a half drive, roughly ninety miles up from the valley at sea level to about two thousand feet in the mountains. Center in the picture is Tom Cutino's chopped '50 Ford. Left is the '31 Ford Model A owned by Arnold Gouveia, and on the right is Jeff Fernandez's '38 Chevy Business Coupe. It is Sunset Red and has had four engine changes since the picture was taken. He still has the car and is planning the fifth engine change soon. It was a very cold day.

Arnold Gouveia's '31 Ford, Tom Cutino's '50 Ford and Jeff Fernandez's '38 Chevy. *Courtesy of Tom Cutino.*

DOWN BY THE SACRAMENTO River where it's a mile wide and cold, Ray Bourdo stands behind his slick 1960 Pontiac Bonneville. He had it painted by George Amaral. He shot a Metal Flake Silver color with purple fading that accented the long lines of the body. It sits lowered with narrow whitewall tires and chrome reversed rims with baby moons hubcaps. Thom Smith's 1954 Chevy is right behind the Pontiac. It's a mostly stock body, painted Mack Truck Orange. He put on chrome reversed rims with baby moon hubcaps. Thom is not in the picture because he was taking the shot. Ray looks like he's freezing!

Thom Smith's '54 Chevy with Ray Bourdo's '60 Pontiac by the Sacramento River. *Courtesy of Ray Bourdo.*

EPILOGUE

If you haven't gone down "the drag" in a hot rod,
you'll never know how great it feels.

The calendar I created eighteen years ago was an effort to document the early years of hot-rodding in the Sacramento Delta area. The cars in it were done by teenagers and young adults who are now mostly people in their seventies and eighties, but a number are not around anymore. I did follow up the calendar with a series of newspaper articles in the local *River News Herald* and *Delta Beacon* to bring attention to the cars in the calendar.

In 1982, I moved out of the area to Chico, a town about 120 miles to the north. It was there that I continued my passion for rods and customs. I found this nice 1957 Chevy two-door hardtop. It was owned by a student at Chico State, and after several visits and offers, he sold it to me. It was on blocks and didn't run, but that is not unusual when buying a twenty-five-year-old automobile, and it's much cheaper. A '57 back in those days went for under $2,000, but today they sell for about $30,000, which is more than ten times as much. I fixed it up with chrome wheels and baby moons and lowered it. The paint job was nice; a Ferrari Red (racing red) paint job and rubbed out and returned to the original brilliance. The engine was rebuilt, and a new exhaust system made it sound good. I kept it for four years and sold it when I moved back to Elk Grove and got $4,000.

I thought that was probably it for me with hot rods, but fortunately, that wasn't the case. I moved to Lodi in 2000, and my friend Thom Smith had previously built a 1934 Ford roadster. It was put together very well, and I bugged him to sell it to me. We were going back and forth on the price when he had an accident on his ranch in Herald and sadly passed away. Later, I was able to purchase the car from his wife, Karen. It wasn't running well, so I brought it home on a trailer and started the transformation to car show condition. That would take quite a while, as everything needed to be redone.

A 1933–34 Ford's style differs from earlier models, which were square-bodied in appearance. The design is an art deco style with lines that sweep to the rear of the car. They were completely different when compared side by side. It is considered a fat fender car in rodding terms because the fenders are separate from the body and extend out and sweep back. The radiator is leaned back, drawing the eye backward to the windshield, a Duvall style, to continue the flow to the trunk and downward to the rear end. The designers at Ford really knew what they were doing; there are few linear lines. This gives the car a sense of motion, and motion is the main primary function of a car.

The engine, it turned out, had a flat lob on the cam shaft and was generally a mess. I bought a brand-new Chevy 350 V-8 and installed it with Edelbrock manifold and four-barrel carburetor. Everything else underneath was rebuilt, including a new Mustang 2 front end. Sanborn Chevrolet body shop in Lodi did the major, off the frame, fitting and assembly. It also prepped and painted it a Chevy Cruise Crystal Red Metallic Tint. It's the nearest thing to Candy Apple Red anywhere. I had a custom interior in tan leather built at Finish Line Interiors in Santa Clara. The company designed and built the seats and trunk to my design. It's finished with polished mag wheels. The finishing touch is what every hot rod needs: flames. Lucky 7 Customs in Antioch laid down the best set I've ever seen, with expert pin-striping by Marcos, the owner. Oh, did I mention that I made a model 1934 Ford roadster when I started the build? Model building has always been an interest of mine.

I have entered my roadster in the Sacramento Autorama (a goal since my youth) and got a second place in my class. Hot August Nights was another bucket list thing I did. Cruising down Virginia Street in Reno was bigger than any I've ever done. There are many shows ahead, large and small, so I'll be looking down the road. I hope it's a very long road!

GLOSSARY

APPLETONS. Usually dummy (not real) spotlights mounted downward so the chrome igloo dome is attached to the top of the fender. If they were mounted upward, they would look ridiculous.

BLOWER. A supercharger that forces high volumes of air through the carburetors. Sometimes they blow up.

CARSON TOP. A custom, made-to-fit top, rigid and upholstered. No one knows who Carson is or where the name came from.

CHANNELING. Cutting the floorboards so the car body sits down lower on the frame rails. Sounds like you steer looking between your knees.

CHOPPING. Cutting the top off and removing sections to lower the roof. Hopefully, they fit back together—mostly they don't.

CONVERTIBLE. Cars with a fabric-covered top with a metal frame, foldable with side windows. The top will disappear into a rear panel and sometimes refuse to return.

COUPE. Two-door car with a roof and rear seat. Not to be pronounced coo-pay, please.

CUSTOM. A vehicle altered from stock. It includes mild-to-extensive changes to the entire car to satisfy the imagination of the owner. There are some very wild customs out there and owners with wild imaginations.

DEUCE. A nickname for a 1932 Ford of any kind. It probably wasn't invented by the Beach Boys.

FADE-AWAYS. Wide fenders that continue back into the body. These were made famous by Harry Westergard, who originated the term long before the NBA.

FAT FENDERS. Round-shaped and wider-than-normal fenders on various cars. They almost take up two parking spots.

FRENCHING. Headlights and taillights sunk lower into the body and smoothly molded in. Probably originated in France.

HARDSHIP DRIVER'S LICENSE. A special license issued to rural underage teenagers to race on paved state highways instead of the dirt roads on a ranch.

HEADERS. Custom exhaust pipes from the engine that collect to a single larger pipe, where all pipes join, each the exact length. They also give the deep-throated roar that scares other drivers and pedestrians.

HIGHBOY. A Model A Ford roadster or coupe that sits high on the frame and has no fenders. It is very cold up high and windy when driving too fast, and there's no heater. Brrrrr!!!

HOT ROD. A hand-built, stripped-down and modified car that is minimal in appearance, lightweight, with a powerful engine that is loud and very fast. Hot rod is a really wild name for a car, and it fits well.

LAKE AND DRAG PIPES. Short or long pipes that run along the rocker panels between the front and rear wheel wells. They run directly from the manifold unmufflered, to reduce back pressure for faster performance and speed. They also make the car lower to the ground and very loud. Very annoying to the people in the back seat.

LEAD SLED. It's a lowered car with extensive body modifications. Lead was the filler used before plastic fillers replaced it. Lead is a dangerous metal when used improperly, and it might make you really sick if you don't drink enough Lucky Lager beer.

LOUVERS. The are vents that are punched, usually in rows, to let heat out of the engine compartment. But everyone knows they really are for making the car look really cool.

LOWERING. Making the car lower to the ground by various means like cutting the coil springs. However, if you cut to many coils out, it's too low and you get tickets from the cops. Then you have to buy new springs and measure better.

MOLDING. Filling in body seams to obtain a smooth finish. It seems that if the seams are not filled in smooth, you would seem to have a problem.

MOONS. Small round hubcaps that cover the circle rim around the lug nuts. They do not moon the other car.

PEAKED. An accent seam that runs down the hood. Wonder what kind of accent it has: "Ah, français."

POST. The pillar that runs between the front and back door of a four-door car. If it was not there the doors would fall off when opened.

POWER PLANT. It's a term used when describing your motor, very powerful. You hope they mistake it for something nuclear.

PROJECT CAR. A vehicle under various stages of construction. It will probably be that way for the next twenty years.

RAKE. You cut the coils and drop the front end to a down angle. It's the same angle you hold your garden rake when raking.

RESTORED. An old car that looks like it was rolling new off the showroom floor. But a hot-rodder restores a car the way it should have looked but didn't.

ROADSTER. A convertible vehicle without a top or side windows. The wind blows in your face, and you look like a dog with its head out the window.

RUMBLE SEAT. A folding seat for two in the trunk compartment. If they fall out, you won't even notice.

STREET ROD. A car or truck built before 1948 that is modified and street legal. They also drive them under the posted speed limit at all times. In accordance with the law, of course.

SUICIDE DOOR. A door that opens forward, into traffic. It's not what you were thinking.

T-BUCKET. A Model T Ford of the 1915 to 1927 era that's fenderless and topless and extensively modified. They have an engine, frame, four wheels and body. That's simple enough but add thousands of dollars and hours to the coolest car just to meet girls.

TUCK AND ROLLED. A custom upholstery with pleats and rolls that form semicircle humps that are uncomfortable to sit on. You have to make sacrifices to look cool.

VIN. Vehicle identification number, a small plaque attached to a vehicle and recorded on the registration form to make it legal. No one records it, and most only need it when they sell the car. It's impossible to find what happened to a car with those numbers. Good luck trying.

WOODY. A vehicle design feature with natural finished and sealed wood that cover parts of a car. It's now a car adopted by surfers, and you can't have one unless you are a surfer. You're out of luck in the Great Plains of America.

BIBLIOGRAPHY

Custom Cars. "Built by Dad…Owned by Daughter." August 1960.

Ganahl, Pat. *Lost Hot Rods II: More Remarkable Stories of How They Were Found*. North Branch, MN: CarTech, 2012.

Hot Rod Magazine. "Build Model Cars." January 2000.

River News Herald. "4 Vehicles Customized by Rio Vistan Win High Honors." March 1, 1961.

———. "Hot Rodders Termed among Best Drivers on Highway by Authority." February 24, 1960.

———. "Tops in Show." March 1961.

Rod & Custom Magazine. "Fast Freight." August 1960.

———. May 2006.

Shelton, Chris. "Second in Line but Second to None." *Rod & Custom Magazine* (2010).

ABOUT THE AUTHOR

John V. Callahan published his first hot rod–themed articles and calendar in 2003 with monthly columns in the *River News Herald*. The series was titled Callahan's Car Corner and featured many of the cars in this book. He attended Riverview Elementary School and Rio Vista High School before moving with his family to Lodi and attending Lodi High School. He entered the U.S. Army and served three years stationed with the Fourth Armored Division in Nüremburg/Fürth, Germany, at Monteith Barracks, as a crewman on an M-60 tank during the Cuban Missile Crisis. After returning home, he attended San Joaquin Delta College and played for the Mustang football team. John

A 1934 Ford Roadster with flames, about fifty-three years later.

worked for United Parcel Service as a driver and in management for thirty years. He then joined California Overnight (now On Trac) and retired there after ten years of service as a corporate manager.

He enjoys bird carving, hot rod building and several volunteer programs in Lodi, including as chairman of the Arts Commission in 2005 and 2006. This is his first published book, using personal experiences and information from many interviews and a vast amount of research.

Visit us at
www.historypress.com
....